# U.F.O.s

# U.F.O.s

## ROBERT JACKSON

SMITHMARK

A QUINTET BOOK

This edition first published in the United States in 1992
by SMITHMARK Publishers Inc.
16 East 32nd Street, New York, NY 10016.

SMITHMARK books are available for bulk
purchase for sales promotion and
premium use. For details write or call
the Manager of special sales
SMITHMARK Publishers Inc.
16 East 32nd Street, New York, NY 10016
(212) 532–6600.

ISBN 0–8317–9056–3

This book was designed and produced by
Quintet Publishing Limited
6 Blundell Street
London N7 9BH

Creative Director: Richard Dewing
Designer: Nicky Chapman
Project Editor: Stefanie Foster
Editor: Rosemary Booton
Picture Research: Liz Eddison

Typeset in Great Britain by
Central Southern Typesetters, Eastbourne
Manufactured in Hong Kong by
Regent Publishing Services Limited
Printed in Hong Kong by
Leefung-Asco Printers Limited

# Contents

Where it all started      6

Shot down by UFOs?      14

Strange things in Earth orbit      20

Lights in the sky      28

Have UFOs been caught?      36

What the pilots saw      44

Seized by flying saucers?      50

UFOs in history      58

The search for other worlds      66

People like us?      72

Index      78

# Where it all began

## It began with Kenneth Arnold

Kenneth Arnold was by no means the first person to witness the phenomenon nowadays called an Unidentified Flying Object, or UFO, but it was his experience that sparked off the wave of UFO hysteria that was to endure throughout much of the 1950s.

It happened on Tuesday, 24 June 1947. Arnold, a businessman from Boise, Idaho, was flying from Chehalis to Yakima in Washington State, piloting his own aircraft. He had been installing fire-fighting equipment for the Chehalis Central Air Service earlier that afternoon, and had overheard someone

BELOW Kenneth Arnold, the businessman from Boise, Idaho, who sighted something strange in the sky near Mount Rainier on 24 June 1947. It was his experience that sparked off the wave of UFO hysteria that was to endure throughout much of the 1950s.

comment that there was a $5,000 reward for any-one locating the wreckage of a US Marine Corps' C-46 transport, lost somewhere in the Mount Rainier area. The possible crash site was some distance off Arnold's intended route, but he decided to make a short detour into the search area; the reward, after all, was a tempting carrot.

As he cruised along at 9,000 feet (2,743m), a sudden flash of light caught his attention. At first, he thought that another aircraft must be in the vicinity, perhaps also involved in the search for the missing transport. He scanned the sky, but could see no sign of it. Then, as he looked to the north of Mount Rainier, he saw something unusual: nine odd-looking aircraft, flying in line astern at 9,500 feet (2,869m) and following a heading of 170 degrees. Every few seconds, two or three of them would dip or change their course slightly, just enough for the sun to catch their reflective surfaces. The strange craft appeared to be crescent-shaped,

with no sign of any tail surfaces. Arnold assumed that they were some new type of jet aircraft. He saw their shape in greater detail as they passed in front of snow-covered Mount Rainier, and now an even bigger surprise was in store; they were not crescent-shaped, but round. They were a long way off – about 25 miles (40km), according to his esti-mate – and so had to be fairly large, perhaps about the size of a DC-4 airliner, in order to be visible. They were also fast. Using the second hand of his wrist-watch, Arnold timed the passage of the discs over a known distance between Mount Rainier and another mountain peak. His initial calculations indicated that the craft were flying at 1,700mph (2,735kmh) – an unheard-of speed for any aircraft in 1947. Even later, when more precise calculations were made, their speed could not be reduced below 1,300mph (2,092kmh).

On landing, Arnold decided to report what he had seen to the FBI, but the local office was closed.

**ABOVE** Mount Rainier in Washington State provided a majestic backdrop not only for Arnold's UFO sighting, but also for several others in the years that followed. The mountain is a 14,410-ft (4,392-m) dormant volcano.

**"From then on, if I was to go by the number of reports that came in of other sightings, . . . I thought it wouldn't be long before there would be one of these things in every garage."**

Instead, he told the media, and the story went out to the world over the wires of the Associated Press. Within hours of its appearance, reports were coming in from all sides from people who claimed to have witnessed similar craft. Arnold himself, besieged by reporters, commented ironically: "From then on, if I was to go by the number of reports that came in of other sightings, of which I kept a close track, I thought it wouldn't be long before there would be one of these things in every garage. In order to stop what I thought was a lot of foolishness, and since I couldn't get any work done, I went out to the airport, cranked up my plane, and flew home to Boise." But the damage had been done. The newspapers now had a blizzard of UFO sightings on their hands, and exploited them to the full. Reporter Bill Begrette coined the term "Flying Saucers".

● ABOVE Kenneth Arnold displays a drawing of the crescent-shaped craft he saw in the vicinity of Mount Rainier. After his sighting, the press was deluged with UFO sighting reports from all over the United States.

# Investigations begin in America

In January 1948, in the wake of this initial wave of sightings, the US Government launched its first official probe into the UFO phenomenon. These were dangerous times: the "Iron Curtain" had descended across Europe, confrontation between the Soviet Union and the Western allies was escalating, and the Russians were known to be developing long-range bombers capable of flying over the Pole to North America. The Americans themselves were engaged in a highly-secret weapons programme, partly involving the development of a new generation of super-powerful nuclear weapons and rocket missiles. This programme, as far as rocketry was concerned, was being conducted with the aid of German scientists, and the Russians were known to have German scientists working for them too. No one knew how far development had progressed inside the Soviet Union, and speculation arose as to whether the UFOs were in some way connected with it.

To make matters worse, the American public was beginning to grow paranoid about the Soviets. Magazines and newspapers carried fanciful reports, often supported by faked photographs, of amazing new Soviet military aircraft. It was said, for example, that they had flown a piloted rocket plane – based on a wartime German design – that could reach a speed of 1,600mph (2,574kmh) and an altitude of 90,000 feet (27,432m). It seemed

● LEFT Fear of military developments in the Soviet Union undoubtedly accounted for part of the UFO hysteria. In the late 1940s the Russians were developing intercontinental bomber prototypes like this Tupolev Tu-85. Its design was based on America's B-29.

ABOVE Many post-war Russian jet aircraft were produced with the help of captured German scientists. This Ilyushin Il-22, which flew in 1947, drew heavily on wartime German technology – but nothing the Russians had could reach a speed of 1,600mph (2,575kmph) at 90,000 feet (27,432m), despite fanciful rumours.

form of alien spacecraft was little more than a germ in the minds of most people; admittedly, there had been an "alien invasion" scare in 1939, when an all-too-realistic radio dramatization of H. G. Wells' *The War of the Worlds* had sent a brief ripple of panic across the United States, but that had soon died out in shame-faced fashion. Since then the public had been sceptical about aliens in general.

They were by no means sceptical about what the Russians might be up to, though, and so the US Air Force (USAF), in charge of UFO investigations, devoted much time and effort to providing rational explanations of the phenomenon. They tried to explain them away as weather balloons, atmospheric conditions or the light of planets such as Venus, magnified by layers of the Earth's atmosphere. It was also revealed that the Americans themselves had been experimenting with saucer-shaped aircraft. One of them, the Chance Vought XF5U-1, had been rolled out in 1946. It was the prototype of a carrier-based fighter; but the problem was that it had never flown.

plausible enough; after all, the Americans themselves had already exceeded the speed of sound with a piloted rocket plane, the Bell X-1, and speeds were being pushed higher all the time.

The US Government's priority, then, was to allay public fears about UFOs, and what they might be. At this stage, the idea that they might be some

RIGHT America's own "flying saucer", the disc-shaped Chance Vought XF5U-1. The prototype of a carrier-based fighter, it was built in 1946 but never flew.

It was the US film industry that implanted the widespread notion that UFOs might be alien spacecraft. It all started in 1951, with the release of a film entitled *The Day the Earth Stood Still.* In this, a flying saucer lands in America, bringing friendly aliens to warn the peoples of Earth against the dangers of modern war. In the following year UFO sightings reached an unprecedented peak – and reports were leaked of sightings by USAF crews, as well as by the general public.

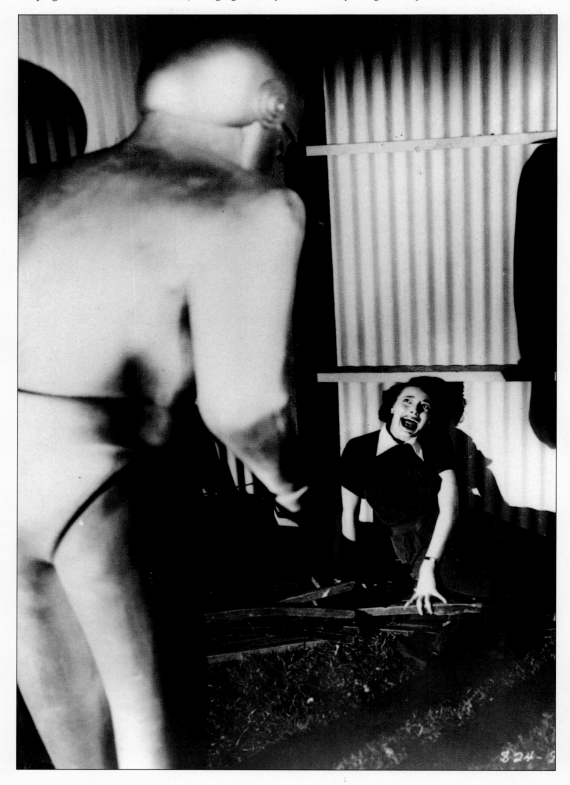

 **LEFT A moment of terror for actress Patricia Neal in the film *The Day the Earth Stood Still.* The film was released in 1951, was a huge box office success, and in the following year UFO sightings reached an unprecedented peak.**

# Sighting over the Gulf of Mexico

At 5.25am on 6 December 1952, Lieutenant Sid Coleman was watching the main radar scope of his B-29 bomber, which was flying over the Gulf of Mexico. Suddenly, the blip of an unknown object, followed by two other blips, appeared on the screen. Coleman checked their speed: it was an incredible 5,240mph (8,431kmh). The navigator also reported blips on his scope. By the time Coleman had recalibrated his set, Captain John Harter had also registered four unknowns.

As a blip approached on the right, another crew member, Master Sergeant Bailey, peered into the night and saw a blue-lit object streak from the front to the rear of the bomber. A second group of blips appeared on all three scopes, followed by a third group. Bending over his screen, the radar

officer saw two UFOs rocketing by on the right. He alerted Staff Sergeant Ferris, who looked out through the waist blister. Instantly, Ferris saw two objects streak by, mere blurs of blue-white light.

Up in the cockpit, Captain Harter saw the UFOs cut across the bomber's course, an estimated 40 miles (64km) away. Suddenly, they turned and headed straight towards the B-29. Then, abruptly, they slowed to the bomber's speed, turned in behind it and kept pace with it for ten seconds before pulling off to one side. At the same moment, Captain Harter saw a huge half-inch blip on the scope, moving at 5,000mph (8,045kmh). The smaller UFOs increased their speed, merged with the larger one, and instantly the huge blip accelerated to 9,000mph (14,481kmh) before disappearing.

⬤ BELOW A Boeing B-29 bomber. On 6 December 1952, the crew of one of these aircraft sighted several UFOs over the Gulf of Mexico. The strange craft shadowed the bomber for several minutes before accelerating away at speeds of up to 9,000mph (14,484kph).

# Civilian airline sightings in the US

A few months earlier, on 14 July 1952, there had been another aerial sighting, this time involving a civilian airliner. At 9.12pm, Pan American pilots First Officer W. B. Nash and Second Officer W. H. Fortenberry were approaching Norfolk, Virginia, in their DC-4 when they saw six disc-shaped UFOs ahead. The UFOs, glowing orange-red, were approaching at fantastic speed in echelon formation. The first disc slowed abruptly, just as if someone – or something – inside it had sighted the DC-4. The next two discs wobbled for an instant, seeming almost to overrun the leader, and then all six suddenly flipped up on edge, changed course violently and streaked away.

The two pilots watched as the discs returned to their flat position, and lined up again in echelon formation. A second afterwards, two other discs raced under the DC-4 and joined the six ahead. Suddenly, all the UFOs went dark. When their glow reappeared, all eight machines were in line. Then they climbed away rapidly and vanished.

A week later, in the Air Traffic Control Center at Washington National Airport, controller Ed Nugent saw seven sharp blips suddenly appear on the main radar scope. He called the tower, where radar

operator Howard Cocklin confirmed that he also had blips on his scope. Later, another controller, Jim Ritchey, saw that a UFO was pacing a Capital airliner that had just taken off. He called the captain, a veteran pilot named "Casey" Pierman, and asked him to investigate. Until then, the UFO's tracked speed had been about 130mph (209kmh). Then, abruptly, it stopped tracking the aircraft. A moment later, Pierman radioed that he had seen the thing, but that it had streaked off before he had been able to get close to it.

● BELOW A DC-4 airliner similar to the one that encountered UFOs over Virginia on 14 July 1952. The UFOs approached the aircraft at fantastic speed before slowing down, changing course and streaking away.

# Trying to explain the phenomenon

The fact that UFOs could be tracked by radar was clear proof that whatever they were, they were solid. The inference was that they were real, and that they could not be explained away as natural phenomena. Often, as in the case of the B-29 crew,

radar contacts were confirmed by visual sightings. This happened again on 5 August 1952, when personnel at the USAF base at Oneida, Japan, saw a UFO carrying a bright white light approaching their base. Watching from the control tower, they made out a dark circular shape behind the glow, about four times the diameter of the light. A smaller, less brilliant light shone from the round, dark under-surface of the strange craft. For several minutes it hovered near the tower, its dark shape clearly visible behind the light, then it accelerated away.

The peak month for UFO sightings in 1952 was April, when at least 100 well-documented reports were made in the USA and Canada. Some of these undoubtedly involved missile tests and fast, high-flying jet aircraft; with the Korean War in full swing the USAF was carrying out a great deal of experi-

● LEFT In the early 1950s, the USAF was carrying out a great deal of experimental flying. Here, an F-84 fighter links up with a B-36 bomber in a long range fighter escort experiment. Could such activities account for sightings of "UFOs joining up with their mother ships"?

● MAIN PICTURE Not a massive flying saucer, but a lenticular cloud formation pictured over Eastern Bohemia. The cloud is formed above a mountain ridge when the wind blows in the direction of the mountain slopes.

● INSETS The cover of the second issue of *Fate* magazine, summer 1948, featuring UFOs. The UFO phenomenon allowed artists to exercise their imaginations to the ultimate degree. Ten years later, the same artistic licence was still running strong. This edition of *Fate* magazine, February 1958, depicts yet another UFO sighting.

mental flying during this period, including in-flight refuelling at night. The aircraft involved, flying high, would display clusters of lights that might appear strange to an uninitiated observer on the ground. Many of the reports also stated that the UFO alternately showed red, green and white lights as it changed position in the sky; the navigation lights of an aircraft are red at the port wingtip, green at the starboard, and white at the tail. Nevertheless, the majority of UFO sightings could not be explained away so easily, and by the end of 1952 the phenomenon was well established throughout the world. Flying-saucer research groups sprang up everywhere, and sightings multiplied in countries other than the United States. With this massive wave of interest, there arose a lamentable tendency to invent UFO stories, or at least to seize on historical events and attempt to "prove" that alien activity had somehow been involved. Eagerly, in their search for evidence of alien contact in past ages, UFO devotees turned their attention to the world's ancient records – in particular the Bible. From now on, UFOs and religion were to follow a closely parallel path.

# Shot down by UFOs?

## The mystery of McChord Air Force Base, Tacoma

At 6.30pm on 1 April 1959, a big four-engined C-118 transport aircraft of the USAF's 1705th Air Transport Wing roared down the main runway of McChord Air Force Base, near Tacoma, Washington, and climbed away into the southern sky. For the four-man crew, this was a routine training mission – so routine that it was virtually automatic. But just 75 minutes later, all four men were dead – and the C-118 was a mass of shredded wreckage strewn across the side of a mountain.

### "Mayday, Mayday! We've hit something – or something has hit us . . . This is it! This is it!"

At 7.45pm, the staff in the control tower at McChord Air Base heard a frantic distress call from the C-118's pilot. "Mayday, Mayday! We've hit something – or something has hit us . . . This is it!" Then there was only silence. The C-118 had crashed into the side of a mountain in the Cascade Range, 30 miles (48km) north-west of Mount Rainier's 14,400ft (4,389m) peak. Air Force crash crews and armed guards raced to the scene and threw a cordon around the widely scattered wreckage. Newsmen and others who attempted to come close

BELOW  A Douglas C-118 military transport aircraft. On 1 April, 1959, an aircraft of this type was destroyed under mysterious circumstances in the Cascade Mountains, not far from Mount Rainier. What brought it down remains a mystery to this day.

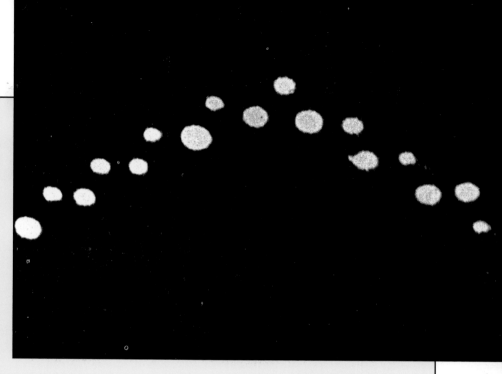

were warned off at gunpoint. Explanations and rumours spread like wildfire. Had the aircraft been testing some new device – hence all the secrecy? Unlikely, as the C-118 was only a freighter. Was pilot error the answer? Or perhaps the C-118 had run into a flock of birds, or had been in collision with a second aircraft.

The Air Force knew that none of these reasons was the real one. A few minutes before the pilot's distress call, the powerful radars at McChord Air Base had revealed that the C-118 had picked up three or four mysterious travelling companions – strange, luminous peaks of light that darted around the big transport. Gradually, the Air Force specialists who were investigating the crash began to build up a minute-by-minute picture of the strange and terrifying fate that had overwhelmed the aircraft and its crew.

At seven o'clock on that April evening, residents in the area between Seattle and Mount Rainier had been alarmed by a series of explosions – mysterious detonations that seemed to come from a clear sky. Twenty minutes later, the whole region was shaken by an even bigger bang. At about the same time, several bright, luminous objects were seen racing across the sky. They travelled at incredible speed and in complete silence. Many other people witnessed strange flashes and glows around the horizon.

Eye-witnesses in Orting, not far from the scene of the crash, told investigators that the C-118 had appeared overhead at about 7.45pm. All the aircraft's four engines were stopped, and a large chunk of its tail unit was missing. But, strangest of all, the C-118 was being followed by a formation of three shining discs. Every now and then, one of them would break away and dart towards the transport, skipping over it and veering off to one side at the last moment. It was just as though the C-118 was being harried by a pack of hounds. Several people in the Orting area had watched the aircraft and its unearthly companions until they were out of sight. A minute later, two bright flashes ripped the sky to the north-east. At that exact moment the radio transmissions from the C-118 ceased abruptly with the pilot's final desperate "This is it!"

Rescue teams arriving at the scene of the crash found a nightmare of charred, twisted metal fragments, hardly any of them more than a foot across, scattered over the whole mountainside. They found three mangled, dislocated bodies, too, sunk deep into the ground by the fearful impact. The fourth body, however, was never found. The aircraft's tail-fin and rudder were discovered much later, miles away in the hills to the north of Mount Rainier.

From the wilderness of torn wreckage, the accident investigators were able to reconstruct exactly how the C-118 had hit the ground, and they came up with a number of facts that baffled them completely. For a start, they calculated that even if the aircraft had nose-dived into the ground under full power, the impact would not have been great enough to rip the machine into such a widely scattered sea of small fragments. But the C-118 had not ploughed into the earth nose-first; it had struck on its belly, as though something had swatted it out of the sky with enormous force.

Whatever conclusions the US Air Force reached, it kept quiet about them, and did its best to lay a smoke screen over the incident. The uncanny story behind the crash first came to light several weeks later, when investigators from a civilian research group known as the Aerial Phenomena Research Organization – which specializes in gathering information on UFO sightings and related incidents – arrived on the scene. Their report was published in May 1959, and caused a few red faces in the USAF's Information Bureau.

Just what really did happen in those last fateful minutes before the C-118's plunge to earth will never be known. There are all sorts of rational explanations for what might have caused the crash; extreme turbulence and "wind shear", which can smack an aircraft out of the sky without warning, are just two. But there can be no rational explanation for the silver discs that seemed to be harrying the C-118 to its destruction.

**ABOVE** The unfortunate C-118 was shadowed by luminous discs like those in this picture. This photograph was taken on 30 August 1951 by Carl Hart Jr. as the UFOs passed over Texas.

# The Kentucky incident

● BELOW Captain Thomas Mantell, Jr, was asked to investigate the strange UFO over Kentucky on 7 January 1948. He climbed in pursuit of it – and minutes later he was dead.

It was in the Mount Rainier area that Kenneth Arnold had seen his strange circular craft skipping around the mountain peaks in 1947, but it was on the other side of the American continent, on 7 January 1948, that another incident occurred which foreshadowed the fate of the C-118 by 11 years. The setting for the January 1948 incident was Kentucky. All day long, the townspeople of Marysville, Irvington and Owensboro and the villages in between had been reporting sightings of a big,

shining UFO, moving slowly and silently across the sky. At 1.15pm, the Chief of Police in Marysville, his office overwhelmed by calls, rang nearby Godman Air Force Base to see if he could obtain any information on the strange phenomenon. The senior air traffic controller at Godman in turn telephoned the Air Force Test Center at Wright-Patterson Field, and was assured that no aircraft of any kind was being tested in the area round Godman Field and Marysville. At 1.35pm, Godman's radar scanners locked on to an "unidentified aircraft" that was approaching the airfield from the south-east at a height of about 13,000 feet (3,962m). Ten minutes later, the controllers picked up the object visually, and saw at once that it was no ordinary aircraft. The thing was shining and circular. It was difficult to estimate its actual size, but it appeared to be about 500 feet (150m) in diameter. It drifted over the centre of the airfield and then stopped, hanging motionless just below the cloud base.

The sky was covered with a layer of cirrostratus (ie uniform) cloud at 14,000 feet (4,270m), through which the sun shone with a pale light. After half an hour, the mystery object shot upwards a few hundred feet until it entered the cloud base. It continued to lurk there, visible now as a hazy, dull-red glow. In the control tower, a heated discussion was going on between the controllers, the base commander, the operations officer, the intelligence officer and several others. They all agreed on one point: the thing up there was not an aircraft or a weather balloon.

At 2.30pm, Godman Tower received a call from the leader of a flight of five P-51 Mustang fighters. They were on a ferry flight, and were about to overfly the field. Godman asked the flight leader, Captain Thomas Mantell, if he would investigate the UFO. At that time, the Mustang flight was about 10 miles south of Godman, and was flying below the cloud base.

Mantell acknowledged, and informed Godman Tower that he was turning on to a heading of 220 degrees and climbing to 15,000 feet (4,570m) in order to intercept the mystery craft. As they passed through 15,000 feet (4,570m), two of the Mustang pilots suddenly broke away and descended. These

aircraft were not carrying oxygen equipment, which in accordance with USAF regulations was mandatory for flights above 14,000 feet (4,270m). Mantell's Mustang was not fitted with oxygen gear either, but he continued to climb, accompanied by the remaining two pilots, Lieutenant A. W. Clements and Lieutenant B. A. Hammond. Their Mustangs both had oxygen, but at 22,000 feet (6,700m) Hammond's supply began to fail and he too broke

**"Jesus Christ, it's fantastic! It's right above me, and it's tremendous! It looks metallic, and it's huge and circular. It could be anything between 500 and 1,000 feet across. It seems to be cruising at about 200 knots, and I'm gaining on it. It's colossal! I'm going to try and get above it. It's climbing! It's starting to climb . . . God, this is fantastic! It's getting hot. It's hot! The heat! I can't . . ."**

away, followed by Clements. Both continued to track the UFO at a lower altitude while Mantell went up to 23,000 feet (7,000m).

At this point, Mantell allegedly radioed: "Jesus Christ, it's fantastic! It's right above me, and it's tremendous! It looks metallic, and it's huge and circular. It could be anything between 500 and a 1,000 feet across. It seems to be cruising at about

200 knots, and I'm gaining on it. It's colossal! I'm going to try and get above it. It's climbing! It's starting to climb . . . God, this is fantastic! It's getting hot. It's hot! The heat! I can't . . ." And then, so the story goes, there was silence.

In fact, Captain Mantell said nothing of the sort. His words were the invention of dozens of lurid newspaper stories that appeared in the wake of the incident. He did say that he had sighted the UFO, that it was above and ahead of him and appeared to be moving at about half his speed, and that it was large and metallic. After that, there were no further transmissions from him. The other Mustang pilots, following the course of the UFO at a safe oxygen level below the cloud, could see neither the object nor their leader. They had tried to warn him about the danger of flying too high without oxygen, but had received no response.

At about 3.15pm, Captain Mantell's Mustang dived vertically into a field on a farm near Franklin, Kentucky, and exploded in a cloud of debris. His body was found in what was left of the cockpit. Some later reports suggested that the remains of the aircraft were "pitted and scored by intense heat", implying that the Mustang had been destroyed by some kind of death ray. Like the spurious contents of the radio transmission, that was not true either; and a post-mortem examination of Mantell's body showed that he had been killed on impact, not earlier.

By the evening, newspapers all over the country had got hold of the story of Mantell's strange and final experience, and the US Air Force felt compelled to issue a statement. The official line was that Mantell, a highly experienced pilot (he was not a fighter "ace", as some reports claimed, but had flown transport aircraft during the war) had been killed when his P-51 exceeded its airframe's structural limits and broke up in mid-air. And the mystery object he had been chasing? Nothing more than the planet Venus, magnified by atmospheric conditions. Astronomers all over the world were no doubt interested to learn that the planet Venus could be picked up by ordinary airfield radar, that it was metallic, up to 1,000 feet (305m) in diameter, and cruised at 200 knots 15,000 feet (4,570m) above the earth. Apparently realizing just how ludicrous this explanation was, the Air Force issued another. This time, they said that Mantell had flown into a meteorological balloon. A weather balloon that cruised around at will all over Kentucky, that hung motionless over an airfield for nearly an hour in spite of high winds at altitude, and then suddenly vanished? Nevertheless, despite all the stories, the weather balloon still remains the official Air Force explanation.

● BELOW The USAF tried to explain the Mantell crash by saying that the pilot had been chasing the planet Venus, magnified by atmospheric conditions. Another "explanation" was that he had flown into a weather balloon.

So what really happened to Captain Mantell? The logical answer is that he suffered anoxia – oxygen starvation – and passed out. The process takes only a few seconds, and the unfortunate aspect is that the afflicted pilot does not realize it

> **"My intentions are to go to King Island . . . That strange aircraft is hovering on top of me again. It is hovering and it's not an aircraft. Delta Sierra Juliet, Melbourne . . ."**

is happening. His aircraft then went out of control, and crashed before he regained consciousness. But what was he chasing over Kentucky that day? That will forever remain a mystery. It must have been something very, very important to make Captain Mantell ignore his years of Air Force training and be oblivious to his own safety. However, the secret of what he really encountered died with him.

So did the secret of what Australian pilot Frederick Valentich saw on 21 October 1978, during what were apparently the last minutes of his life. Twenty-year-old Valentich was flying a Cessna 182 from Melbourne's Moorabbin Airport to King Island, off the coast of Victoria, when he encountered what at first sight seemed to be a large aircraft flying over Bass Strait a few minutes after seven o'clock in the evening.

It was soon apparent that the object was not an aircraft. Metallic and shining, and showing what Valentich described as a green light to Melbourne Air Traffic Control, it buzzed his Cessna at high speed and then hovered overhead.

Valentich told Melbourne that his engine was beginning to run roughly. Melbourne asked him what his intentions were. "My intentions are to go to King Island . . . That strange aircraft is hovering on top of me again. It is hovering and it's not an aircraft. Delta Sierra Juliet, Melbourne . . ."

And that was all. After that last transmission, Frederick Valentich and his Cessna, callsign Delta Sierra Juliet, simply vanished. No trace of either was ever found.

# Strange things in Earth orbit

## The mystery satellite of the North and South Poles

The discovery, when it was made, caused consternation in the United States Defense Department; and no wonder. One of the North American Air Defense System's tracking radars had picked up what appeared to be a huge space satellite in orbit around the earth.

What worried the Americans was that the satellite had not been launched by either the United States or the Soviet Union. For a start, it was in the wrong kind of orbit. The mystery satellite's path took it over the North and South Poles, whereas the orbits of satellites launched from the Soviet Union were invariably inclined at 65 degrees to the equator, which took them over South America and North Africa. Quite apart from that, there was no booster rocket in existence at the time – February 1960 – that could possibly have been powerful enough to put such a satellite into orbit. American space scientists had calculated that its weight was around 15 tons (15.25 tonnes). For three weeks, the Americans kept the satellite under surveillance; then it vanished, as mysteriously as it had appeared.

● BELOW Earth – the home of all mankind. This fantastic view of our home planet was taken by the crew of the Apollo 17 spacecraft during the final lunar landing mission in the Apollo programme. The scope of the photograph extends from the Mediterranean Sea to Antarctica.

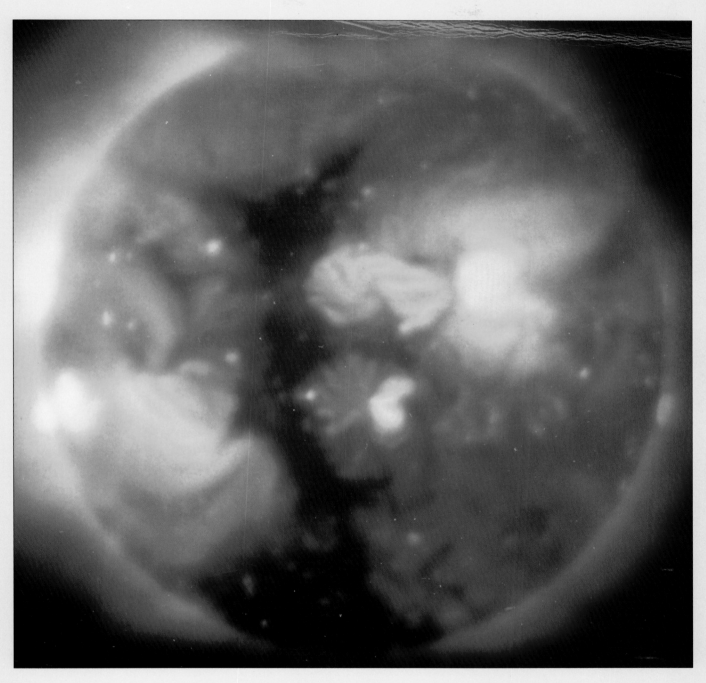

ABOVE This picture of the sun was taken by the Solar Telescope of Skylab. First seen in X-ray pictures, scores of bright points of light dot the solar disc, like scattered jewels. The glittering points are found all over the sun.

The "mystery satellite" of February 1960 was the first in a whole series of strange space phenomena which have been baffling scientists all over the world for three decades. On 3 September 1960, seven months after the first sighting, it was revealed that an unidentified object had been photographed in the sky over New York by a tracking camera at the Grumman Aircraft Corporation's Long Island factory. The object, which appeared to give off a reddish glow, had been seen several times during the preceding two weeks. It was apparently follow-ing an east-to-west orbit, whereas most satellites were launched in the opposite direction, and its speed appeared to be about three times that of America's Echo 1 "metal balloon" satellite.

The Americans attached so much importance to these mystery satellites that they set up a special committee to gather as much information as possible about them. But the committee's findings – if indeed there were any at all – were never made public, and the whole affair was forgotten for the time being.

# Sightings by US astronauts

● BELOW Astronaut Edward H. White, the first American to walk in space, saw something strange and unexplained in Earth orbit. He and James McDivitt took photographs of it – photographs that were never released.

Then, on 15 May 1963, a Mercury capsule carrying Major Gordon Cooper blasted into space from Cape Canaveral on a 22-orbit journey around the world. During his final orbit, the astronaut informed the tracking station at Muchea, near Perth in Australia, that he could see a glowing, greenish object ahead of him. It seemed to be approaching the spacecraft, and it was travelling very fast. Whatever Cooper saw, it was solid, because it was picked up by

Muchea's tracking radar, travelling east to west. Cooper's sighting was reported by the National Broadcasting Company, which was covering the flight step by step, but when Cooper landed, reporters were told that they would not be allowed to question him about the incident. Cooper, it was hinted, might have been hallucinating; on the penultimate orbit an electrical short in the capsule's system had started a series of malfunctions that blew poisonous carbon dioxide back through the astronaut's helmet. But Cooper himself was a firm believer in UFOs; 10 years earlier, he had sighted one while piloting an F-86 Sabrejet over western Germany.

In June 1965, astronauts Ed White – the first American to walk in space, who was later to die tragically along with Gus Grissom and Roger Chaffee in an Apollo space capsule blaze on the ground – and James McDivitt were passing over Hawaii in their two-man Gemini spacecraft when they saw a weird-looking metallic object some distance away. The thing appeared to have long arms or projections sticking out from it. McDivitt took pictures of it with a cine-camera – pictures that were never released.

The official US Air Force explanation was that the astronauts had seen America's Pegasus satellite, which was equipped with broad, protruding "arms" to register hits from micro-meteorites. But the Air Force had ignored one important point: when White and McDivitt were over Hawaii, Pegasus had been more than 1,000 miles (1,600km) away.

In December 1965, Gemini astronauts James Lovell and Frank Borman also saw something strange in space during the second orbit of their record-breaking 14-day flight around the world. Borman reported that he had located an unidentified spacecraft some distance away from their capsule. Gemini Control, at Cape Kennedy, suggested that perhaps he was seeing the final stage of the huge Titan booster which had hurled him and Lovell into orbit earlier that day.

Borman confirmed that he could see the spent booster rocket all right, as it was shining brilliantly in the sun. But what he was looking at now was something entirely different – something he could

JAMES A. McDIVITT

not explain. Later, NASA claimed that Borman had seen the wreckage of a US Air Force rocket that had blown up during a launch several days earlier, but the Air Force themselves scotched that explanation. They emphatically declared that there was no rocket wreckage in that particular orbit, although, admittedly, the USAF was putting a series of military reconaissance satellites into orbit at the time, and these activities were surrounded by the utmost secrecy.

● **ABOVE** Ed White pictured during his historic space walk.

● **LEFT** James A. McDivitt, who was with White in the Gemini capsule at the time of their close encounter with a mystery object.

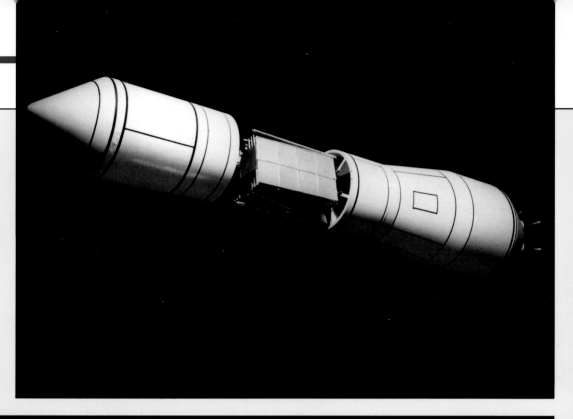

■ RIGHT The Pegasus satellite on the final stage of its booster rocket. This was what the USAF said White and McDivitt had seen – but it was over 1,000 miles (1,600km) away at the time.

# Strange activities in the Soviet Union

■ RIGHT Lt Cdr James Lovell who, with Frank Borman, also sighted an unidentified object in orbit during their record-breaking 14-day Gemini flight around the world. It may have been a secret military reconnaissance satellite.

There may have been a rational explanation for all the sightings in the US. There was certainly one behind waves of UFO hysteria that gripped certain parts of the Soviet Union in the 20 years or so before *Glasnost*.

In June 1980, for example, a great crescent-shaped UFO streaked over the skies of central Russia, glowing bright red. It was seen by hundreds of thousands of people, many of whom panicked in the belief that American nuclear rockets were descending on them. In the days that followed, the mysterious object received a lot of press coverage in the USSR. Some of the more way-out pseudo-scientific journals – of which there are quite a number in Russia – even hinted that aliens had been seen in the streets of Moscow and other Soviet cities.

But it wasn't just the Russians who saw the strange object. An hour later, it was sighted by people in Chile, Argentina, Brazil and Uruguay – still crescent-shaped, but apparently much smaller now and not glowing so brightly. By now, the object was being tracked by the big radar scanners of the United States Air Defense Command, and they showed it up for what it really was. The thing that had terrified half the population of the central Soviet Union was nothing more than a Cosmos military reconnaissance satellite – or rather, the rocket that launched it.

LT CDR JAMES LOVELL

The RD-107 booster rockets that launch Russia's military satellites consist of 20 rocket engines, strapped around a central body to provide a massive initial thrust and acceleration. Once this has been achieved, the boosters are jettisoned and stage two takes over, increasing the acceleration to orbital velocity. When they are all firing together, the clusters of rocket motors that surround the base of the launch vehicle produce an odd effect. Instead of the long ribbon of fire that trails in the wake of America's space boosters, the Russian hardware produces a brilliant crescent-shaped flame that pours from the rocket exhausts as the launcher thunders into the sky.

This is what the Russians saw on that night in June 1980, following the launch of the Cosmos satellite – one of 17 launched that year – from Kapustin Yar, north of the Caspian Sea. The booster rocket's north-east trajectory, inclined at 71 degrees to the equator, took it over Sverdlovsk and across the vast wastes of Siberia. What the peoples of South America saw, an hour later, was probably the second stage of the launch vehicle re-entering the atmosphere and burning up.

For years, flying saucer scares were carefully fostered in the Soviet Union by the state security organization, the KGB, to divert attention from what was really happening in so-called "sensitive areas". For example, anything unusual seen in the skies around Sverdlovsk – a town barred to all foreign visitors because it is an important centre of missile production – was attributed to UFO activity.

## Experts Convinced...
## Dazzling UFOs Caused Mysterious Power Blackouts

Dazzling UFOs which lit up the night skies over Honduras have been linked by experts to two mystifying power blackouts which plunged the capital city into darkness.

Hundreds of eyewitnesses – including government officials – were terrified by the strange glowing objects.

And a Honduran professor openly admits he believes the power losses are due to a "controlled force" that could have come from "extraterrestrial life."

On Oct. 14, 1978, a bizarre, boomerang-shaped UFO was sighted swooping through the sky only a few seconds before power was knocked out for 25 minutes.

Just two weeks later, on October 27, a brilliant, octopus-shaped UFO appeared — and the sightings of this strange craft also coincided with a massive electricity failure of 1 hour and 10 minutes.

The Honduran government officially attributes the power losses to children's kites getting tangled in the power lines. But many people — even some in government — scoff at that theory.

"That's absurd," snorted Dr. Salvador Pardo, dean of the school of engineering at the National and Autonomous University of Honduras. "Kites could not have caused this damage.

"The power went out and then came back — without repairs," he stressed. "This to me makes it obvious that a controlled force caused this blackout. It is perfectly logical to assume that extraterrestrial life could have caused the blackouts."

Added Lieut. Alexander Her-

### By MEL LUNA

nandez, commandant of the Police Officers Academy at Tegucigalpa, the capital city:

"The kite theory is a joke. I personally have seen UFOs in the past here."

Prof. Jose Bercian, director of the program for technical education for the Honduran government, told The ENQUIRER that he, too, had seen a UFO — on September 26.

"What appears to me is that a UFO swept down the high tension lines for whatever reasons and sucked up the power," he said.

As for his own encounter, Prof. Bercian added that while driving at about 2 a.m. September 26, he and his wife had spotted a "glowing globe" that descended rapidly and landed just off the road. "I slowed down and wanted to take a close look," he recalled. "But my wife was terrified and wouldn't let me."

Major Honduran newspapers and TV and radio stations have

**SHE SAW IT:** Donatila Hernandez Mojan points to where UFO hovered over substation.

been flooded with hundreds of reports of UFO sightings dating all the way back to September.

Radio America, one of the country's most popular radio stations, received as many as 200 calls the night of October 27.

"All described the object in exactly the same manner — an octopus-like object showing a brilliant light," commented Radio America news director Rodrigo Wong.

The first blackout, on October 14, was linked to a very different UFO.

"I noticed a V-shaped or boomerang-like object hovering over the airport about a kilometer (half a mile) away at an altitude of 500 meters (1,650 feet)," remembered Rogelio Bercian, director of publicity for La Tribuna, and a brother of Prof. Bercian.

"Suddenly I saw the UFO dive over the airport at an incredible speed and the entire city went black. I later saw this object soaring up in figure-eight maneuvers before it disappeared."

But even more spectacular was the incredible glowing ob-

ject with tentacles of blinding light that coincided with the power outage of two weeks later.

"It looked like an octopus with moving tentacles," remembered taxi driver Roberto Aguilar. "As it swept down into the valley — boom! — all the lights went out."

Herman Badgette, press secretary to the Honduran military junta, was standing on the terrace of the Maya hotel in downtown Tegucigalpa with Associated Press correspondent Tom Fenton.

"I saw a large, bright ball of light," Badgette remembered. "From the white center of the object, multicolored rays of light descended downward.

"Some were blue and red. They looked like bolts of lighting. It disappeared at great speed."

Turns Alberto Aguilera, a

**BERCIAN**   **LOPEZ**   **AGUILERA**

**ABOVE** Late in 1978, a series of dazzling UFOs appeared in the night sky over Honduras, in Central America. They are said to have caused mysterious power blackouts. Could they have been connected with Russian satellite launches?

**LEFT** A massive solar flare erupting from the sun. The white dot to the right of the photograph represents the Earth, shown to the same scale. Such flares release a cosmic ray bombardment that can produce curious phenomena in the Earth's upper atmosphere.

In 1979, there were reports of intense UFO activity over the mountainous areas of Kazakhstan, north of Tashkent. There is a lot of nomadic activity in that area; despite frequent attempts by the Russians to seal their southern frontier completely there has always been a considerable movement of native tribes through the mountains that separate the Soviet Union's southern republics from India and Pakistan, so it was not long before reports of strange "lights in the sky" had spread over a wide area. It was then that Soviet newspapers began to carry stories of UFOs being sighted over Kazakhstan and its neighbouring republics. What was actually happening, however, was much more down to earth.

The mountains of northern Kazakhstan conceal one of the most top-secret installations in the Soviet Union. It is sited at Sarishagan and is cut off completely from the outside world. There, within a giant scientific complex that includes 12 high-energy particle generators, the Russians were – and still are, despite recent political events – engaged in what the US Central Intelligence Agency has code-named Project Tora; the race to produce laser and particle beam weapons capable of knocking out enemy satellites or the warheads of incoming missiles. Whenever experiments were carried out, a mysterious glow could be seen for miles around, lighting up the sky over the secret complex. Because of the security blanket that surrounded Sarishagan, the Russians could afford to ignore any local speculation about what caused the glow. But when the stories of what was going on at the complex began to spread farther afield, they invented a deliberate cover involving UFOs.

It may be that reports in the Western press sparked off KGB interest in UFOs. Western newspapers and journals were combed diligently for scientific information, and the Russians must have quickly realized that UFO sightings around the world often coincided with the launch of spacecraft from the USSR's northern cosmodrome at Kapustin Yar. The inference was clear: the "UFOs" were, in fact, the various stages of the Soviet booster rockets. So flying saucers became part of the KGB's arsenal of deception, and the Soviet security service received unexpected help from the people themselves. The Soviets love science; millions of them are science-fiction addicts, and seize eagerly on anything that seems a little out of the ordinary. And even if the KGB-sponsored UFO reports failed

to dupe all the people for even a fraction of the time, at least they helped liven up the columns of the newspapers.

Oddly enough, there are few reports about UFO sightings by Soviet cosmonauts in space. This is odd, because the Soviets have amassed far more "space time" than their American counterparts. However, in the 1960s one story about a Soviet space sighting did the rounds.

It involved the Soviet spacecraft Voskhod 1, which went into orbit on 12 October 1964 carrying a crew of three. Its commander was Colonel Vladimir Komarov, who was killed in April 1967 when his Soyuz-1 capsule plunged to earth under unopened parachutes. When Voskhod was launched, the Soviets stated that it was intended to remain in orbit for a "considerable length of time". But it was brought back to earth, under conditions amounting to panic, after only 24 hours.

The story, current at the time, was that recordings of radio transmissions between Voskhod and mission control had indicated that the spacecraft's crew had seen something strange and inexplicable in orbit – something that terrified them so much that they made a hasty and unscheduled descent from space. The truth was much more mundane: the Voskhod launch was little more than a propaganda stunt; it was the first time that a three-man crew had been placed in orbit. But the cosmonauts were crammed into a capsule designed for one person, with no spacesuits, no emergency escape-system, and only minimal life-support in the way of oxygen and supplies.

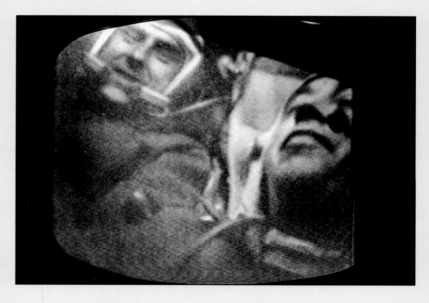

● **BELOW** Colonel Vladimir Komarov, seen on the left of the photograph, inside the Voskhod 1 spacecraft on 12 October 1964. Komarov was killed in April 1967 when his Soyuz 1 capsule plunged to earth under unopened parachutes.

RIGHT Soviet cosmonaut Alexei Leonov was the first man to walk in space. On one space trip, he landed off course in the Ural Mountains after an unscheduled departure from orbit. He was reported to have encountered "something strange".

When the spacecraft was ordered back to earth prematurely, Komarov asked for an extension, which was refused. Quoting from Shakespeare's *Hamlet*, Sergei Korolev, head of the Russian space programme, told the spacecraft commander: 'There are more things in heaven and earth, Horatio, than are dreamed of in your philosophies.' That remark, monitored by Western observers, gave rise to speculation that Voskhod's crew had seen something out of the ordinary. The speculation increased when, instead of proceeding straight to Red Square for the customary official reception, the three cosmonauts were placed in quarantine for several days.

When they finally arrived in Moscow, they discovered the real reason behind Korolev's quotation, their rapid exit from space, and their enforced isolation. While they were in orbit, Premier Nikita Khrushchev had been ousted from power. His successor was Leonid Brezhnev, who had decided to mark his first public appearance as the top man in the Kremlin by staging a triumphant welcome for the returning cosmonauts.

# Lights in the sky

## Wanaque Reservoir, New Jersey

The night of 11 January 1966, was bitterly cold. Patrolman George Dykman pulled up the collar of his fur-lined jacket and shivered as he gazed out across the frozen six-mile (9.6km) expanse of Wanaque Reservoir in New Jersey, 50 miles (80km) from New York. Despite the cold, Dykman had to admit that the scene was peaceful. No sound disturbed the silence, and reflections of starlight glimmered on the reservoir's icy surface.

**BELOW** Mysterious green fireballs depicted on the front cover of *Fate* magazine, June 1957.

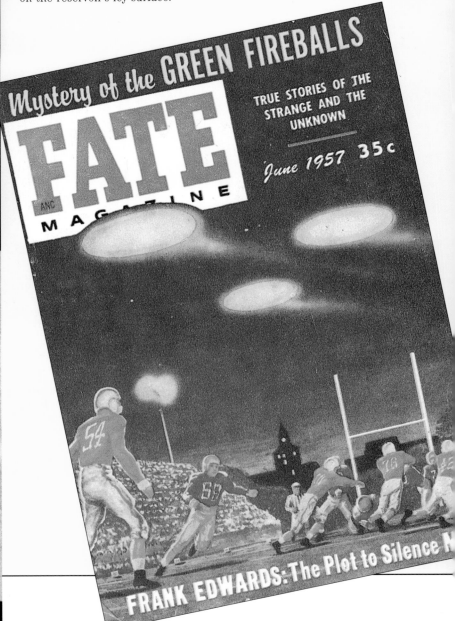

Mystery of the GREEN FIREBALLS

## FATE MAGAZINE
AND

TRUE STORIES OF THE STRANGE AND THE UNKNOWN

June 1957  35¢

FRANK EDWARDS: The Plot to Silence

Suddenly, something caught Dykman's attention. At first, he thought that it was an aircraft; but then he watched in amazement as the object grew in size, turning into a brilliant white light. It was flying very slowly, cruising over the northern end of the dam. As he watched, its colour turned to red and then to green, and finally back to white again. Dykman had seen enough. Running back to his car, he switched on the radio and alerted other reservoir police patrols. Within minutes, several of his colleagues had arrived on the scene and were gaping in astonishment at the glowing thing that still hovered above the ice.

Other witnesses had seen the strange object, too. They included the Mayor of Wanaque, Harry Wolfe, his 14-year-old son Billy and two members of the city council. Soon, a crowd of people had gathered on the banks of the reservoir. The "craft" shone with a reddish light now, and was cruising backwards and forwards just above the ice. As far as the watchers could estimate, the object was about 10 feet (3m) in diameter. It shone with a constant, unwinking glow, and moved in a curious swaying flight rather like a pendulum.

Abruptly, the object climbed a few hundred feet and became stationary. From it, a brilliant beam of light – like a searchlight, only much thinner – flashed down onto the ice. The light continued to

flash on and off at intervals for the next hour. Then, without warning, the object began to gather speed and climbed steeply. A minute late, it was lost among the stars. The crowd of people was just beginning to disperse when more cars roared up, filled with newspaper reporters and photographers. A few of them continued to hang around hopefully for another couple of hours, but at about 1.30am they packed up their gear and went away, bitterly disappointed. Only two policemen, brothers Joe and Dave Cisco, were left to watch the spot.

Just 30 minutes later they radioed that the mysterious light was back again and that they were watching it through binoculars. It looked different this time, like several brilliant stars clustered together in a tight group. After a few minutes it darted away and they lost sight of it.

Early the next morning, reservoir officials went out to inspect the ice. At the northern end of the reservoir, at the spot over which the UFO had hovered, they found that the water was welling up through a number of near-circular holes. It was as if they had been melted through the ice by a huge blowtorch. During the nights that followed, mysterious glowing objects were sighted over and around Wanaque several times. Their colours ranged from white to a brilliant blue, and witnesses reported objects either circular or egg-shaped.

**ABOVE** This UFO, a luminous disc, was photographed over Paris, France, at 3.45am on 29 December 1953 by engineer Paul Paulin. During the two-minute exposure, the UFO "jumped" sideways and then became stationary again.

The next major sighting occurred in March, when a low-flying UFO terrified nuns at Saint Francis Convent, not far from Wanaque. There were several sightings throughout that summer, but it was not until October 1966 that the UFOs returned to Wanaque Reservoir in force. On 12 October, at least 10 people saw a "flying saucer" hovering over the reservoir. It was like a flat disc, with a rounded dome on top, and seemed to be made of some kind of metal that resembled aluminium. It was first sighted by Sergeant Thompson, a reservoir police officer, who was so startled by the object's brilliant light that he almost drove his car into a tree. The UFO came down low enough over the reservoir to stir up the water in its wake.

By this time, the story was making headlines all over America. Wild theories were put forward to account for the UFO's apparent interest in the reservoir; someone suggested that the waters of reservoirs all over the world were being systematically doped with tranquillizing drugs, so that the Earth could be taken over by invaders from space without a fight. Another theory was that the UFOs actually had a base beneath the waters of Wanaque.

Towards the end of 1966, besieged by a flood of enquiries from all quarters, officials at Stewart Air Force Base near New York issued an explanation. The mysterious flying objects of Wanaque, they said, were nothing more than brightly lit-helicopters. A few days later, apparently realizing just how ridiculous this explanation must have sounded to those who witnessed the UFOs, the Air Force came up with another gem – a standard old faithful, this time. The lights, they said, were the planet Venus. As one of the reservoir policemen told reporters, when the planet Venus comes close enough to stir up the waters of a reservoir in North America, it's time for everyone to start worrying.

**BELOW** These mysterious lights in the sky were photographed by a coastguard at Salem, Massachusetts, Air Station in August 1952. He watched them for several seconds as they dimmed and brightened in what appeared to be a regular pattern. The lights were also seen by several colleagues.

**RIGHT** The silver object in this picture was photographed over Bulawayo in what was then Southern Rhodesia (now Zimbabwe) on 29 December 1953 – the same day that a similar phenomenon was seen over Paris.

# An unearthly power in Sweden

Several years before the Wanaque incident, on 20 December 1958, two young Swedes allegedly had an unnerving experience with mysterious, unearthly lights. Stig Rydberg and Hans Gustafsson were driving home through dense fog to spend Christmas with their families when, on a stretch of main road between Hoganas and Helsingborg, they saw a strange, pulsating light among the trees that lined their route. Puzzled, Rydberg pulled the car over to the side of the road and stopped. The two men decided to investigate. Shivering in the chill dampness of the fog, they left the car and began to walk cautiously through the trees towards the weird light.

Suddenly, the men stopped short as a strange, frightening sight met their eyes. In a clearing, a glimmering, diffuse light hovered a few feet above the ground. It seemed to surround a vague, indistinct object. The next instant, the men recoiled in terror. Drifting rapidly towards them, out of the glow, came a cluster of what could only be described as "blobs". They were about three feet (one metre) across, and they gave off an "alien" grey-blue light. Before the two men could move, the blobs were all around them. Gustafsson cried out in fear as a sudden terrifying pressure seized them. Slowly, step by step, an unseen force began to push them towards the pulsating glow.

The two men retched as a frightful stench enveloped them. It was like burnt meat. Rydberg flailed his arms desperately, lashing out at the hovering blobs. His hand plunged deeply into one of them; it was like hitting a quivering jelly. Abruptly, a thin whistling noise split the air. It grew in intensity until the men clasped their hands over their ears in pain. The sound seemed to tear at the very fibre of their brains, destroying their will to resist.

Suddenly Gustafsson stumbled against something, the shock jolting him back to his full senses. It was a post, the remains of an old fence. He grabbed it with both hands and hung on grimly. At once, the terrible force exerted even greater power. To his utter horror, Gustafsson felt his feet rising from the ground. Within seconds he was stretched out

⬤ **BELOW LEFT** This drifting luminous disc was photographed by Christian Lynggaard at Vaerlose Air Force Base, Denmark. The photo is quite genuine.

⬤ **BELOW RIGHT** When Mr M. R. Lyons of Nottingham, England, developed the film he had taken in the Derbyshire Peak District in the early summer of 1972 he got a surprise – this ball of hazy light a few inches in diameter appeared on it. He had seen nothing at the time.

stumbled towards the road through the undergrowth and hurled himself into the car.

Trembling with shock and fear, Rydberg started the engine, eager to put as much distance as possible between himself and the terrifying thing in the forest. As he did so, a shrill whining sound cut through the fog. Slowly at first, the pulsating glow in the trees began to rise. Then, gathering speed, it shot upwards until its light was lost in the murk.

It wasn't until three days later that the two young Swedes told anyone about their horrifying experience. They had agreed to keep quiet about it for the simple reason that people would have said that they were either drunk or crazy. But try as they might, they could not shake off the frightful stench that had almost overpowered them in the forest. It clung to them, seeming to grow even stronger as

horizontally, his legs waving in mid-air and pointing towards the glowing object. He gritted his teeth and clenched his hands still more firmly around the post.

The force seemed to be concentrating on Gustafsson, and suddenly Rydberg found the pressure lifted from him. He turned and ran towards the car. Looking over his shoulder in fear, he saw that two of the blobs were drifting after him. Branches whipped at his face as he ran as fast as he could through the fog. Reaching the car the now frantic Rydberg tore open the door and jabbed his hand down on the horn.

The sudden harsh blare had an astonishing effect on the blobs. For an instant they wavered, and then they began to drift back towards the glowing thing in the clearing. Gustafsson – still clinging desperately and horizontally to his fence-post – fell to the ground with a thud. Scrambling up, he

the days went by, making their stomachs heave with sickness. As last, in desperation, they went to see a doctor. The doctor could find nothing wrong with them, but they were so obviously distressed that he urged them to make a full statement about their experience. During the next few days they were interrogated and examined by police, Swedish defence officials and psychiatrists. None of their interviewers seemed entirely convinced that the two men were telling the truth – until they were subjected to deep hypnosis.

Finally, Rydberg and Gustafsson offered to take the defence experts to the place where they had seen the thing in the clearing. They found no spacecraft and no flying blobs of jelly, but they did find three deep marks in the soft ground, apparently made by some sort of landing gear. The experts examined the area, made notes, and then stamped "Unexplained" on the case file. And, except in the nightmares of two young men, the whole business was forgotten.

● **ABOVE AND RIGHT** UFO photographed by Hannah McRoberts north of Kelsey Bay, Vancouver Island, British Columbia, Canada in October 1981. She was photographing the mountain, and neither she nor her companions saw the UFO. The second photograph is a section of the original, concentrating on the mystery object.

# A rational explanation – Woodbridge, England

A great many UFO sightings, both in the sky and on the ground, involve lights rather than solid, recognizable objects, and often there is a rational explanation behind such events. In October 1983, for example, the world's popular newspapers ran a story on an alleged "close encounter" between extra-terrestrials and personnel at the USAF base at Woodbridge, in Suffolk, England. It all began with a headline in a British national Sunday news-paper that screamed "UFO LANDS IN SUFFOLK – AND THAT'S OFFICIAL!"

In fact, all that had happened was that a US Air Force colonel reported having seen a strange light in nearby woods. A ranger from the Forestry Commission turned up to investigate and demonstrated that the strange light could only have been the rotating beam of the Orford Ness lighthouse, five miles (8km) away, flickering through the trees.

● LEFT Japanese news photographer Tsutomu Nakayama took this UFO photograph in Hawaii on 25 April 1974. He never saw the UFO, which did not appear in other photographs of the scene. This is an enlargement of part of the photo.

# "Foo Fighters" – balls of light

Then there are the strange, drifting balls of light that frighten the occupants of aircraft from time to time. In 1987, Eastern Airlines flight EA539 was climbing over New York City a few minutes after midnight when a bright electrical discharge suddenly enveloped the aircraft. In the cabin, a startled passenger looked up to see "a glowing sphere a little more than 8in (20cm) diameter which emerged from the pilot's cabin and passed down the aisle of the aircraft". Its colour was blue-white, with an almost solid appearance. It glided along at walking pace about 30in (75cm) from the floor.

**"a glowing sphere a little more than 8in (20cm) diameter which emerged from the pilot's cabin and passed down the aisle of the aircraft".**

Allied bomber crews reported similar phenomena during World War II, and dubbed the mysterious balls of light that drifted slowly through their aircraft "Foo Fighters". In the post-1947 wave of UFO hysteria, the light balls assumed great significance. It was widely believed that they were reconnaissance robots sent out by an alien mother ship in orbit to keep an eye on the warring tribes of Earth, and to gather information on the interiors of their primitive fighting machines.

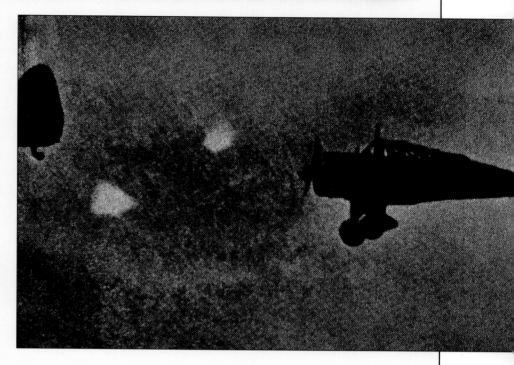

● **ABOVE "Foo Fighters" with a pair of US Army Air training aircraft.**

● **BELOW UFO photographed by Ella Louise Fortune on 16 October 1957 as it hovered over Holloman Test Range, New Mexico.**

What the so-called "Foo Fighters" are, in fact, is a manifestation of ball lightning, one of the more bizarre scientific riddles of our time. A typical ball is about 10in (25cm) in diameter and glows a pale red or orange colour. It may have a halo, or corona, around it, and sometimes it emits sparks or rays. These balls materialize literally out of the blue, or perhaps out of the clouds. They can last for a minute or more before extinguishing. The mode of their demise varies: some explode violently, while others just fade away.

For some reason, the glowing balls "prefer" interior spaces, seeking out the insides of aircraft and buildings. They seem to react in some way to nearby objects, especially if those objects are made of metal. Sometimes they emit a menacing hiss or crackle, and exude a sulphurous smell.

A sulphurous smell – that could, perhaps, be confused with the smell of burnt meat? Was it a form of ball lightning that Rydberg and Gustafsson encountered in a Swedish forest? And did it generate a powerful force field that almost tore them from their feet? The ways of UFOs may be strange, but the natural phenomena of our own planet can sometimes produce stranger effects.

# Have UFOs been caught?

## Silence over Spitzbergen

The pilot of the Norwegian Air Force Catalina flying boat was bored. For over four hours now, as the aircraft droned deeper into the long Arctic shadows, he and his crew had seen nothing but a vast expanse of grey sea and white ice-floes, lit only by an occasional flash of dim, sunlight that lent a delicate shade of pink to the great ice-pack off Norway's North Cape.

It was May 1952, and the Catalina was on a routine ice-survey mission from its base in northern Norway. Ahead of the aircraft now, and to the right, the jagged snow-capped peaks of Spitzbergen rose

**BELOW** The military in the United States and other countries spent a great deal of time and effort searching for UFOs that were reported to have crashed. This cover of *Fate* magazine, May 1954, depicts such a search.

**FATE** MAGAZINE

SPECIAL SAUCER ISSUE

*May 1954*

35¢

HUNT FOR THE SAUCERS

A DOCTOR HEALS BY FAITH     I KNEW A WITCH

ABOVE Traces of an alleged UFO landing site, protected by stones, at Socorro, New Mexico, USA, on 24 April 1964. The circular impression in the ground could be attributed to various causes – including people.

from the icy sea. The pilot turned the Catalina slightly, bringing it over the island's western shores. Dwarfed by the mountains that towered above it, the aircraft cruised on. Another half an hour or so, and it would be time to set course for home. Suddenly, a flash of reflected light caught the pilot's eye. There was something down there, glittering among the crags. Skimming past a sheer mountain wall, the pilot brought the Catalina down for a closer look. Whatever had caught his attention appeared to be metallic. The long polar shadows made it difficult to make out the exact shape of the object, but it looked like the crumpled wreckage of a crashed aircraft. If it was, there might be survivors. In that freezing climate, there was no time to waste in getting help.

The Catalina climbed away from Spitzbergen, its radio operator flashing an urgent signal to the Norwegian Air-Sea Rescue Service. Within half an hour, rescue teams were on their way to the island by air. But as the Catalina flew homewards, its crew was unaware that their discovery on barren Spitzbergen was destined to become one of the biggest mysteries of modern times.

A few days later, the Norwegian Government released an amazing statement to the newspapers. It claimed that the object found on the island was, incredibly, the wreck of a flying saucer – a disc-shaped craft that was definitely not of this earth. The statement also said that a thorough investigation and analysis of the alien object was being carried out by Norwegian, British and American experts. Journalists from all over the world flocked to Norway, seeking more information; but the Norwegian Government refused to make any further comment. After the initial earth-shaking announcement, there was only silence and complete secrecy.

The silence was broken very briefly a few months later, when an un-named United States Air Force spokesman told newsmen that the mystery craft had been of Soviet origin, and had carried Soviet markings. The newspapers were by no means satisfied but they filed the story as unusable through lack of reliable information and forgot about it.

Then, in September 1955, the Norwegian Government revealed that a Norwegian General Staff Board of Inquiry had practically completed an investigation into the nature of the mystery object, and was about to make its findings public. The Chairman of the Board, Norwegian Air Force Colonel Gernod Darnbyl, stated emphatically that the wrecked craft could not have originated on Earth. The materials used in its construction were completely unknown, and had defied every attempt at analysis. Therefore the statement that it was of Soviet origin was false. Furthermore, a detailed examination of the disc

had revealed certain technical features that were beyond the grasp of terrestrial science.

Colonel Darnbyl went on to say that a team of Air Force specialists – who had been keeping a close watch on the Arctic regions since the crashed disc was discovered – had formed the opinion that the area within the Arctic Circle was being used as a base by alien craft. The specialists had logged a great deal of UFO activity during their three years of surveillance. The statement concluded that the true facts behind the affair were of sensational importance, and should be made known to the public without delay. The full report would be published after discussions with the US and British Governments.

But the report was never published. One of Norway's NATO partners – either the USA or Britain, or maybe both – had apparently clamped down on the release of any further information. Both the USA and Britain, at that time, were classifying UFO information under the heading of "secret".

So the mystery of the Norwegian UFO remains. Was it really an alien spacecraft that was found wrecked on Spitzbergen, and were its remains secretly spirited away to be examined behind locked doors? Or was there a more plausible, but equally secret, explanation behind what was found in the Arctic Circle?

Early in 1952, USAF reconnaissance aircraft were undertaking regular flights inside the Arctic Circle from bases in the United Kingdom. These aircraft, mainly giant Convair RB-36Ds, were gathering photographic intelligence on bases in the northern Soviet Union – and in particular on the island of Novaya Zemlya, where the Russians had built a new nuclear test centre.

One RB-36D is known to have been lost in 1952 while engaged on these clandestine missions. Was it its wreckage that was discovered on Spitzbergen – and was the flying-saucer story a deliberate invention to cover up the true details of what the Americans were doing? The question remains unanswered, but the fact remains that there are other cases where the wreckage of UFOs has allegedly been found, and the evidence rapidly removed.

● **OPPOSITE** Police examining an alleged UFO landing trace near Richmond, Virginia, on 21 April 1967.

● **LEFT** Ludvig Lindbäck, whose brother Knut witnessed the event, points to the spot in Lake Kölmjärv, Sweden, where a UFO crashed on 19 July 1946. The object was possibly a V-2 type rocket, test launched by the Russians from a captured German installation on the Baltic coast.

● **BELOW** The wreck of a crashed USAF B-36 bomber. Was it the remains of a secret reconnaissance version of this aircraft that was discovered on Spitzbergen?

# The UFO in the Peropava River, Brazil

According to one account, a UFO that crashed in a river in South America may still be there. In the afternoon of 31 October, 1963, nine-year-old Ruth de Souza was playing with some young friends not far from her home on the banks of the Peropava River, in Brazil's Sao Paulo province, when she was startled by a strange roaring noise. Looking up into the sky, the children shrank back in fear. Moving slowly towards them at tree-top level was a shining disc, and it seemed to be losing height as it moved towards Ruth's house. Suddenly, there was a loud thud as the object collided with the trunk of a tall tree that stood in its path. The disc wavered, then changed course and moved out over the river, rocking violently. It seemed to be struggling to gain height. Then, abruptly, it plunged into the water like a stone and vanished. Mud and debris came bursting to the surface amid an explosion of huge bubbles. The river seemed to be boiling at the spot where the disc had disappeared.

Ruth's mother, Senõra Elidia Alves de Souza, had also been startled by the roaring sound. She came out of the house and ran to where the children were staring at the churning water. A minute later Ruth's uncle, Raul Alves also arrived at the scene. Like Elidia, he had heard the noise but had not seen the object. Utterly perplexed, he could give no answer to the children's questions. He drove to the nearby town of Iguape and reported the incident to the police. Although sceptical, they agreed to send officers to the scene.

Fortunately for the children – whose story might easily have been casually dismissed as a figment of childish imagination – some fishermen on the opposite bank of the river had also seen the flying disc. They said that the thing had been about three feet (1m) thick and between 15 and 20 feet (4.5 and 6m) in diameter. Somehow – perhaps because of its roar – they had got the impression that the disc was immensely powerful. It had been very

bright, like highly polished aluminium. Its movements had suggested to the fishermen that it was not manned, but was operated by some form of remote control.

The water at the point where the disc had crashed was about 12 feet (3.5m) deep, but beneath it was a 15-foot-thick (4.5m) layer of silt. The witnesses agreed that the disc had plunged into the water with sufficient force to bury itself deep in the mud. It had been heavy, too; the investigators found that a great gash had been torn in the trunk of the tree which the disc had struck during its erratic flight.

**ABOVE AND RIGHT** These remarkable pictures depict a UFO photographed over Trinidad Island in the South Atlantic on 16 January 1958. The UFO appears to have a flat disc encircling its main body.

ABOVE Photographs of UFOs over the British Isles are comparatively rare. This one was snapped by Stephen Darbishire at Coniston in Cumbria's Lake District on 4 February 1954.

The police marked the exact spot where the disc had plunged into the river. By that same evening, every newspaper in Brazil had got hold of the story, and the following day hordes of curious sightseers and UFO investigators descended on the peaceful Peropava. Strangely enough – possibly because the disc had not come down in a military area – the Brazilian defence authorities showed no interest in the incident.

On the morning of 2 November, a diving instructor named Caetano Iovanne, with the assistance of two colleagues, made an attempt to recover the disc. For several hours they searched the murky river bed, probing here and there among the thick layer of mud, but they found no sign of the mystery object.

The next day, a second attempt was made by another team of divers, using special search equipment. They also drew a complete blank. All they succeeded in doing was to stir up large amounts of mud, which made conditions on the river-bed even more impossible than before.

Several more attempts were made over the next few days. Mine detectors were used to sweep the river-bed in the hope that they might reveal some trace of the metal object buried in the mud – but the thing had either sunk too deeply in the silt, or it had disappeared altogether. Someone suggested that it might have been washed downstream, but because of its perceived size and weight this was unlikely. Another theory was that it had moved downstream under its own power. If the disc really was some kind of spacecraft, it was even possible that it had been retrieved secretly during the night. Possible but improbable, for any activity would almost certainly have been seen.

The most likely conclusion is that the disc is still there, buried deep in the mud at the bottom of the Peropava. And the secret of its true origin will doubtless lie buried with it forever.

# UFO or nuclear deterrent – Roswell, New Mexico

There have been several other reports of crashed UFOs. On 2 July 1947, for example – only a week after Kenneth Arnold's famous sighting – a large UFO allegedly exploded in mid-air near Roswell, New Mexico, and scattered a considerable quantity of debris over a ranch owned by William Brazel. US Air Force investigators, alerted about the incident, collected as much of the wreckage as they could find. It was loaded on to an aircraft and flown to Carswell Air Force Base near Fort Worth, Texas, even though other bases were closer to hand; these included Roswell Air Base itself, which was then the home of the 33rd Fighter Group, equipped with P-51 Mustangs.

So why was Carswell selected as the wreckage's ultimate destination? The choice is interesting. Carswell was a principal base of the newly created United States Air Force Strategic Air Command, which in 1947 was building up to become America's strategic nuclear deterrent force. Whatever crashed at Roswell – despite all the publicity that later surrounded the incident – was almost certainly something to do with Strategic Air Command's activities. A major air exercise was in progress at the time; Strategic Air Command was carrying out its first "maximum effort" mission, with hundreds of B-29 bombers carrying out simulated attacks on major metropolitan areas. It might not have been a

● RIGHT In the mid-1980s, aliens were reported to have landed in the Soviet Union. This picture shows an "alien spacecraft" tucked away in a Russian hangar. The whole affair belonged to the realms of science fiction.

● BELOW A flight of UFOs photographed over Conisbrough, Yorkshire, England, by Stephen Pratt on 28 March 1966.

**Scientist's grim warning: Soviets will use alien technology against us!**

RUSSIAN HANGAR holds this amazing intergalactic craft. The alien starship, with its incredible technology, will give the Russians new superweapons!

appear to be sexless, have no mouths and are covered with tiny, flesh-colored scales.

And while there is no indication that the Soviets have succeeded in communicating with the aliens, Dr. Wolff

only a matter of time before they do.

"The Soviet report notes that the extraterrestrials can read minds so we believe that communication is not only

craft because the report says they flew it from Siberia to Moscow or the new day the

Dr. Wolff. "We also know that the Soviets have figured

B-29 that came down at Roswell, but it might have been something secret that fell off one. As for the mid-air explosion, there was a thunderstorm in progress at the time, and a simple thunderclap could have accounted for that.

There were quite a few "crashed UFO" stories in the hysteria years of the late 1940s and early 1950s. Most of them were pure invention on the part of people who wanted to leap on to the UFO bandwagon. Some are harder to dismiss, but on close investigation turn out to have logical explanations behind them. One is left with the inescapable conviction that tales of intact UFOs being retrieved by "the authorities", along with the bodies of alien crew members, belong firmly in the realms of science fiction.

**ABOVE** This UFO photograph, date unknown, was taken in Denmark. There is a strong possibility that it is faked.

# Strange lights over Granada

It was a beautiful night; the sky was crystal clear, with a full moon. In the streets, people looked up curiously as a roll of thunder split the warm stillness. High above their heads, four sets of twinkling navigation lights raced across the sky and vanished in the halo of radiance around the moon.

In the cockpit of the Portuguese Air Force F-84 Thunderjet there was complete silence, except for the muted whisper of the slipstream and the hum of electrical equipment. Captain José Ferreira was conscious of the beauty of the night too, but he had little time to enjoy it. He was preoccupied with the task of navigating his aircraft accurately.

⬤ The cover of *Fate* magazine (left), dating from April 1957, shows a US jet fighter attacking a UFO. In reality, no such interception was ever made. Flying saucers featured heavily in the magazine during 1957. The depiction of a UFO encounter appeared on the front cover in August (below).

## U.S. JET ATTACKS SAUCER!

TRUE STORIES OF THE STRANGE AND THE UNKNOWN

## FATE MAGAZINE

April 1957 35¢

I HAVE SEEN ZOMBIES

## SAUCERS OVER EUROP

BY AIMÉ MICHEL

## FATE MAGAZINE

August 1957 3:

ALL ABOARD FOR THE MOON
By FRANK EDWARDS

# What the pilots saw

**The flying saucer is 40 years old, but no-one is throwing a party**

# I see no spaceships!

## There's a UFO cover-up say skywatchers

By ANDREW McKENNA

THE flying saucer is 40 years old this week, but the UFO department of the Ministry of Defence won't be holding a party.

The department consists of one civil servant, a notepad and a filing cabinet.

The solitary official logs UFO reports in the notepad and then uses the filing cabinet in which to dispose of them.

"They're all filed" explains the MoD, which means they are never heard of again.

"If we had a report of a UFO hovering over a Cruise missile base, for instance, we would investigate. We're only interested in a military connection.

"We have heard nothing to suggest that UFOs are in any way hostile and we still have no proof they are from outer space."

This is how far we've come since pilot Kenneth Arnold spotted nine bizarre objects zig-zagging over the mountains on America's west coast on June 24 1947.

He described them as "a chain of saucer-like things" and Pressmen dubbed them 'flying saucers'.

Arnold wrote a book called 'The Coming of The Saucers' and they've been coming ever since.

The trouble is that no-one knows what they are, who's in them and where they're coming from.

Not only saucers can fly. Thousands of reports from across the planet list flying cigars, triangles, rectangles, spheres, blimps, tops, and lights.

UFOs, which have been recorded since ancient times, have been spotted by airmen, pilots, doctors, business executives, farmers, police, servicemen and former US president Jimmy Carter – not just by people walking dog at closing time.

A new survey says that one in six of us has had a Close Encounter of the First Kind (which means we've seen something odd in the sky)

But officialdom's reaction has been to shrug its shoulders, smile gently and proffer a list of 'explanations'.

In 40 years these have included clouds, meteors, aircraft, ball lightning, lighthouses, tricks of the light, reflections, the planet Venus, alcohol, hallucination and, amazingly, badgers.

Tell that to the fighter pilot who chased a UFO the size of a Boeing 707 across the skies above Tehran in September 1976.

He described it as an intensely brilliant object with flashing lights. Suddenly a smaller bright object descended from it and rushed towards him at unbelievable speed.

He attempted to fire a missile, but all his weapons and communication systems suddenly failed.

The smaller object rejoined the 'mother ship' which landed on the ground casting a glow up to two miles around it.

The report comes not from Steven Spielberg, but from the CIA.

It was kept secret until the enactment of the Freedom of Information Act.

UFO buff Richard Lawrence of the London-based Aetherius Society says: 'Over the past 40 years we've seen a great UFO cover-up by world authorities.

'The society, which believes many UFOs are literally out of this world recently obtained a wad of reports from the US which reveal an official cover-up of an airline pilot's UFO sighting over Alaska.

'Such unearthly behaviour is common,' Lawrence reckons.

**There's one! A UFO photographed by a bank employee in Warrington, Cheshire, in 1978**

● **ABOVE** A Republic F-84 Thunderjet, the type flown by Portuguese Air Force pilots when they had a frightening encounter with UFOs on the night of 4 September 1957 during a routine cross-country navigation exercise.

● **INSET** This UFO was allegedly photographed by a bank employee in Warrington, Cheshire, in 1978. Defence departments in the USA and UK have been accused of "covering up" UFO reports; in fact, no such cover-up exists.

It had been 7.20pm on 4 September 1957, when Captain Ferreira and the three other Thunderjets of his flight had streaked down the runway of Ota Air Force Base, Portugal, on the first stage of a routine night cross-country navigation trip. The other three pilots were all sergeants: Manuel Marcelino, Alberto Covas and Alberto Oliveira. The four jets climbed steadily until they reached 25,000 feet (7,260m), then they levelled out and settled down on the flight towards their first turning-point, the Spanish town of Granada. Granada's lights twinkled on the horizon, right on schedule. Overhead, the four jets made a gentle turn until they were heading back towards the Portuguese border and their second checkpoint, the town of Portalegre.

It was then that Ferreira noticed something unusual – a brilliant, pulsating light away to port,

hanging low over the horizon. The flight commander called up the other pilots; they had seen it, too. As they watched, the light seemed to glow with a multitude of colours: reds, blues and dazzling greens. Suddenly, it grew larger until it was about six times its original size; then, just as abruptly, it dwindled into a faint yellow pinpoint. Whatever it was, it seemed to be keeping pace with the Thunderjets.

At 10.35pm Captain Ferreira ordered his flight to abandon the planned exercise and execute a 50-degree turn to port. When the turn was completed, Ferreira looked for the mystery object, and saw that it had moved too. It was still directly over on his left, and it must have moved pretty fast to get there. There was now absolutely no doubt that the orange light was shadowing the F-84s.

The object, which was giving off a reddish glow, looked about the size of an orange. It was impossible to tell how far away it was. Although it was still keeping station with the jets, it had descended until it was well below their 25,000–foot (7,620m) altitude. For another 10 minutes, it followed the jets without changing its course, colour or size – and then, as the pilots watched, something incredible happened. One after the other, four small yellow discs broke away from the red object and took up an impeccable formation on either side of it.

All at once the red UFO, which appeared to be about fifteen times bigger than its companions, shot upwards in a fast climb straight towards the jets. Captain Ferreira shouted into his microphone, ordering his pilots to break formation. Opening his throttle, he pulled the Thunderjet around in a hard turn, trying to cross the path of the climbing UFO. In his windscreen, a point of light grew bigger with frightening speed. It was one of the smaller UFOs. It loomed up in Ferreira's gunsight, resolving itself into a flat disc. Instinctively, Ferreira jabbed his thumb down on the gun button, then remembered that the six machine guns of his Thunderjet were not armed. The next instant, the UFO sped overhead in a hazy blur and vanished.

Ferreira's earphones crackled with shouts as the other pilots desperately tried to avoid the hurtling UFOs. The discs were incredibly fast and manoeuvrable: no man-made object could move like that. The UFOs rocketed upwards in a vertical climb and disappeared in seconds. Breathing hard, Ferreira called up his excited pilots over the radio and brought his widely scattered flight back into formation. A few minutes later the pilots landed safely at their home base, shaken but none the worse for their uncanny encounter.

> **"Please don't come out with the old explanation that we were being chased by the planet Venus, weather balloons, or freak atmospheric conditions. Whatever we saw up there was real, and intelligently controlled. And it scared the hell out of us."**

When the pilots' report was eventually released, a local weather observatory came up with an interesting piece of information. At precisely the time when Ferreira's pilots were tangling with the UFOs over the Portuguese border, the observatory's sensitive equipment had registered unaccountable variations in the Earth's magnetic field – a common occurrence in areas where UFOs are sighted.

Captain Ferreira and his pilots were convinced that the objects they had seen were not of this world. And later, when Ferreira was telling his story to Portuguese Air Force investigators, he said: "Please don't come out with the old explanation that we were being chased by the planet Venus, weather balloons, or freak atmospheric conditions. Whatever we saw up there was real, and intelligently controlled. And it scared the hell out of us."

# Sightings by RAF and USAF personnel in the UK

A similar occurrence, this time in daylight, also frightened Flight Lieutenant J. R. Salandin of the Royal Air Force on 4 October 1954. In fact, he was so shaken by his experience that he had to fly around for a further 10 minutes before he could pull himself together sufficiently to tell Control what he had seen.

Salandin, a pilot with No. 111 Squadron, RAF Fighter Command, had taken off from North Weald in Essex in his Gloster Meteor jet fighter at 4.15pm. Climbing towards two other aircraft which he could see above him, he was surprised to see two small objects, one silvery and the other gold, pass nearby. Salandin had hardly recovered from his surprise and was still wondering whether he had been the victim of a hallucination when he happened to look straight ahead – and received one of the biggest frights of his flying career.

Straight towards him at tremendous speed was a disc-shaped object. In the brief time Salandin had for observation, the thing appeared to have a flange in the centre and two bulges above and below this. It was so near that it overlapped his windscreen. A collision seemed inevitable. Then, at the last moment, the object swerved and flashed past on the Meteor's port side.

There have been a number of instances where UFOs have been recorded on the gun-camera film of fighter aircraft. The camera is activated when the pilot presses the firing button and, as well as in actual combat, is used to record "kills" during simulated dogfights. The Operations Record Book of No. 43 Squadron RAF tells of one incident in 1955, when two Hawker Hunter jet fighters were engaged in mock combat high over the North Sea. When the gun-camera film of the attacking Hunter was screened at the exercise de-briefing, it showed a ball of bright light, that appeared to be solid, drifting slowly into the frame. The ball hung there for several moments, appearing to be pacing the two aircraft, and remained poised about half-way between them before drifting away again. Neither pilot had seen anything.

**BELOW** This UFO was photographed at 12,000 ft (3,657m) by Shinichi Takeda of Fujisaw, Japan. The object appeared to be shadowing the airliner in which the photographer was travelling.

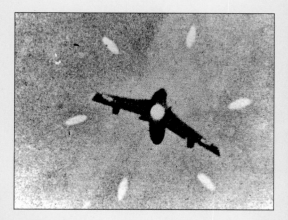

**ABOVE** A Hawker Hunter jet fighter of RAF Fighter Command is captured in the gunsight of another during a combat exercise. On one occasion in 1955, a UFO appeared on the gun-camera film of a Hunter dogfighting over the North Sea.

The Royal Air Force never paid a great deal of attention to UFO sightings; they were duly recorded in squadron operations record books, and sometimes became the subject of "special occurrence reports", but that was all. Not unnaturally, the Air Ministry (Ministry of Defence (RAF) from 1960)

● LEFT The elongated fuselage of an aircraft in flight can sometimes be mistaken for a UFO under certain light conditions. It would not be difficult, for example, for these B-36 bombers to appear as something out of the ordinary at a distance. The B-36 served with the USAF at the height of the "flying saucer" era.

● BELOW A de Havilland Venom night-fighter, the type that chased a UFO over much of East Anglia on the night of 13 August 1956. The Venom's radar operator reported that the UFO was capable of fantastic speeds.

received frequent requests from members of the public, asking for information about the UFO phenomenon; the official line was one of "no comment", simply because there was no firm evidence to comment on. This led to speculation that the ministry was involved in some sort of dark and sinister "cover-up", but in reality there was never anything of the sort.

Neither was there a deliberate cover-up in the United States, where the whole UFO question was treated far more seriously by the USAF. Although UFO sightings were given a "secret" classification for many years, at the height of the Cold War, so were many other happenings involving the military.

The USAF's investigation into UFO sightings by both military and civilian pilots was carried out in a programme code-named Project Sign, which was downgraded in 1949 and its name changed to Project Grudge. In 1951 the name was changed yet again, this time to Project Blue Book, and its coverage expanded to include all UFO sightings. By the end of 1953 more than 4,000 sightings had been logged, but about half these were very unreliable and the Blue Book investigators evolved a system whereby witnesses were graded according to age,

observational experience and so forth. Reports from pilots naturally continued to receive high priority, and there were plenty of them.

One extraordinary case, on 13 August 1956, involved a joint effort between the USAF and RAF in an attempt to intercept a UFO. At 9.30pm, radar operators in the Ground Controlled Approach (GCA) unit at the USAF base of Bentwaters, near Ipswich in Suffolk, detected something odd about 30 miles (48km) out over the North Sea. It was heading inland, and closing at a phenomenal speed, covering six miles (9.5km) with every four-second sweep of the radar antenna. The incredulous controllers worked out its velocity at close on 5,000 miles per hour (8,000kmh). At the same time, more radar targets were picked up at a range of 8 miles (13km), also moving towards Bentwaters. Between 12 and 15 echoes were approaching in a cluster, preceded by three more objects in triangular formation. The pilot of a Lockheed T-33 jet trainer belonging to the 512th Fighter Intercepter Wing at Soesterberg in the Netherlands, who was heading for Bentwaters on a night navigational sortie, was asked to investigate but saw nothing.

The cluster continued its passage, increasing the range to around 40 miles (64km), then merged to form a single, very powerful radar echo. It remained stationary for nearly 15 minutes, moved

off to the north-east, stopped again for a few minutes, then gathered speed and vanished from the radar scope.

The original, single radar target, meanwhile, had merged with ground echoes and been lost. But at ten o'clock another single blip – or perhaps it was the same one – appeared on Bentwaters' radar, crossing the screen at an estimated 4,000mph (6,400kmh). A strange object was also detected on radar at nearby Lakenheath, also a USAF base in Suffolk. HQ 3rd Air Division, controlling all USAF units in Britain, was alerted, and so was RAF Fighter Command, which was responsible for the air defence of the British Isles. The alert now passed to the RAF Ground Controlled Interception (GCI) radar complex at Neatishead, Norfolk, about 40 miles (64km) north-east of Lakenheath. The GCI controller there was authorized to scramble an interceptor.

That night, it was the turn of No. 253 Squadron of the RAF's No. 11 Group to man the night-fighter "battle flight" in East Anglia, with the crew – pilot and radar observer – of a de Havilland Venom NF.2 strapped in their cockpit and ready to scramble at a moment's notice. When the call came, the Venom was quickly airborne and heading towards the target detected by Lakenheath radar. Meanwhile, at RAF Waterbeach, No. 253 Squadron's base, a second Venom night-fighter crew was brought to cockpit readiness.

The radar operator in the first Venom established contact with the UFO and steered the pilot on a course to intercept. The target was now stationary, and the Venom rapidly came within gun range – at which point the radar operator lost contact. It was hardly surprising: both Lakenheath and Neatishead informed the Venom crew that the UFO was now behind them and keeping pace with them as their aircraft circled.

For the best part of 10 minutes the Venom pilot did his best to shake off the UFO, but it clung doggedly to his tail, remaining at a distance of about 200 yards (180m). In the end, the pilot broke away and headed back towards Waterbeach; the UFO followed him for a while, then stopped. It eventually began to move again, heading north at 600mph (965km), and vanished from Lakenheath's radar screens at a range of about 60 miles (96km). The Second Venom was scrambled, but its crew never made contact with the mystery object.

# Huge flying walnut between Iceland and Japan

What occurred over East Anglia that night remains just as much a puzzle as the strange object that shadowed a Japan Airlines Boeing 747 freighter for 30 minutes in January 1988. The 747 was flying from Iceland to Japan via Alaska when its crew sighted the object, which was described by the aircraft captain, Kenju Terauchi, as "very big, about twice the size of an aircraft carrier". He said that it closed to within five miles (8km) of the aircraft, and asked US air-traffic controllers for permission to take evasive action if necessary. The controllers confirmed the existence of a large blip on their radar screens, and said that it might have been composed of three separate objects flying close together. To the 747 crew, it looked like a huge flying walnut. The US Federal Aviation Administration launched an investigation, but came up with no answers.

● **BELOW** This photograph is an enlargement of the mystery object that appeared to shadow a Martin B-57 jet bomber during a test flight from Edwards Air Force Base, California, in September 1957.

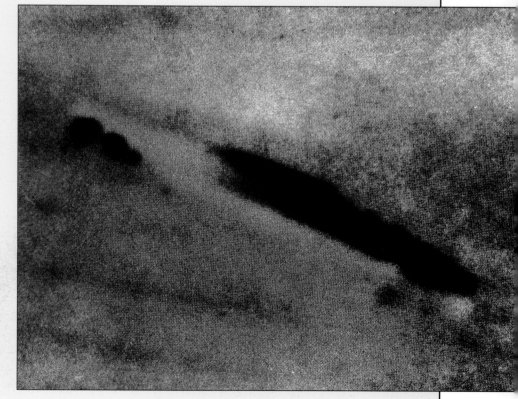

# Seized by flying saucers?

## The first "contactees"

It was perhaps predictable that, very shortly after Kenneth Arnold's UFO sighting triggered off the flying-saucer explosion, people would come forward and claim actually to have travelled in alien craft, either as willing "guests" of the spacemen or as abductees. Most of these tales can be dismissed as pure invention, and in this respect the biggest inventor of all was the self-styled "Professor" George Adamski, who probably did more damage to serious UFO study than any other individual.

A Polish immigrant to the United States, Adamski earned a living serving hamburgers in a local café and lived a few miles from Hale Observatory on Mount Palomar, which then had the world's largest telescope. He styled himself an authority on mystical matters and esoteric Eastern religions, and the

● BELOW The late George Adamski, who claimed to have first met "space people" in the California desert in November 1952 and to have been given rides in their spacecraft. He later lectured on his experiences and on "cosmic philosophy".

advent of the flying-saucer wave opened up a whole new world for him. He claimed to have seen UFOs in 1946 – but only made the claim after Kenneth Arnold hit the headlines a year later – and, in two subsequent books, claimed to have met alien beings from Mars, Venus, Jupiter and Saturn, all of which were, apparently, pretty good places on which to live and nothing at all like the pictures of them painted by astronomers. He stated that the other side of the Moon, too, which was used as a base by aliens, had been turned into a green and fertile place, with plants flourishing under artificial domes. Adamski had seen it all for himself, having been taken for a ride in flying saucers. His two best-selling books also took the public for a ride, and he made a lot of money out of them. Adamski was lucky in that he hit the flying-saucer "jackpot" before American and Russian spacecraft revealed Mars to be a cratered desert, Venus to be a burning, sulphurous hell-hole, Jupiter and Saturn to be freezing gaseous balls of hydrogen and methane, and the hidden face of the Moon to be even more inhospitable than the face turned constantly towards the Earth.

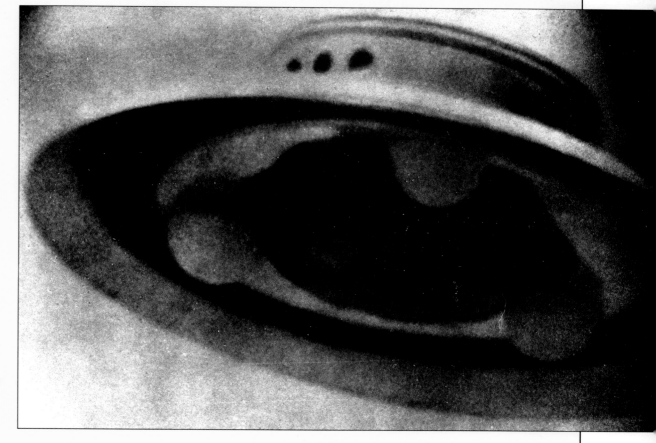

● RIGHT "Flying saucer" said to have been photographed by Adamski in Palomar Gardens, California, on 13 December 1952. The "alien spacecraft" is in fact a clever model.

Apart from bringing down a certain amount of ridicule on the UFO question, Adamski's claims were little more than harmless nonsense, and at this distance in time his works can be read with some amusement. He was the first of the "contactees", but he was by no means the last. Another, Howard Menger, went one better; he not only established contact with an alien, he married one. Later, he discovered that he was really a Saturnian named Alyn who had been reincarnated in the body of an Earthling.

Adamski, who died in 1965, was probably the most charismatic "contactee" figure; the only person to come anywhere near him in terms of notoriety was a Swiss farmer named Eduard "Billy" Meier who, in the 1970s, published a series of photographs which purported to show alien spacecraft from the Pleiades star system. He attracted a considerable following in Europe, and his farm became a place of pilgrimage for Ufologists from all over world.

⬤ **ABOVE** Howard Menger and his wife Connie, who was said to be of alien origin. Menger later claimed that he was a reincarnated Saturnian named Alyn.

⬤ **LEFT** Eduard 'Billy' Meier, second only to Adamski in terms of UFO notoriety, pictured at his Swiss home. The portrait on the wall features his extraterrestrial friend, Semjase.

# Barney and Betty Hill

UFO abductions first came to prominence in 1966 with the appearance of a best-selling book, *The Interrupted Journey,* by John G. Fuller. It recounted the experiences of Barney and Betty Hill, a couple from Portsmouth, New Hampshire. According to the story, they were driving home along US Route 3 after a trip to Niagara Falls when a bright object appeared and hovered over the road. As it drew nearer, they could see that it had a row of windows along its side. Through them, they could see figures which appeared to be in uniform moving about. When the Hills got home, distraught and confused by what they had seen, they found that they could not account for the two and a half hours after the sighting. They had no recollection at all

of this period. Betty began having nightmares about being subjected to a kind of medical examination by aliens, and she and her husband suffered from growing anxiety problems. In the end, they went to Boston psychiatrist Benjamin Simon, who placed them under hypnosis and questioned them about their experience. To his surprise, they shared a very detailed "memory" of being carried aboard the UFO by men with oriental, cat-like eyes and grey faces, who subjected them both to painful physical examinations.

The Hills' experience, when it became public knowledge, unleashed a flood of similar stories across the world, and resurrected interest in earlier abduction or attempted abduction stories.

ABOVE Barney and Betty Hill, who claimed to have shared an unnerving and terrifying experience after being abducted by alien beings as they drove home from Niagara Falls. Their story never faltered, even when they were under hypnosis.

# The experience of the Sutton family

One of the more dramatic of the abduction stories – and one of the few to be reported to the US Air Force at the time – involved the Sutton family of Hopkinsville, Kentucky, and received considerable publicity at the time.

In the evening of 21 August 1955, 16-year-old Billy Sutton had just stepped outside his father's farmhouse to get a drink of water from the well when he saw a bright, circular object hovering over the farm buildings. As he watched, it dropped down out of sight. Billy ran indoors and told the rest of the family what he had seen. His father, Elmer Sutton, shrugged his shoulders and thought that it had probably been a "shooting star"; it was the time of year when the richest annual meteor shower, the Perseids, crossed the Earth's orbit and produced a brilliant display as they burned up in the atmosphere. He gave the matter no further thought until an hour later, when his dogs began to bark furiously, a sure sign that some stranger was outside. Elmer and his eldest son, John, went to the door and peered out into the gathering darkness – and what they saw gave them the fright of their lives.

There, about 50 feet (15m) away from the farmhouse, crouched an unearthly creature. It looked like a small man, less than four feet (1.2m) in height, and it gave off a weird, luminous glow. It seemed to be wearing a suit of some shiny material. Mrs Sutton, who had been looking over the men's shoulders, gave a gasp of fear as the being, with the gait of a monkey, began to move slowly towards the farmhouse. The family stood rooted to the spot in terror as the creature came closer. They could make out more details now: a bulbous head that seemed far too large for the tiny body, and a pair of long, flexible arms ending in webbed hands that seemed to have what looked like gleaming talons attached to them.

Twenty feet (6m) away, the creature stopped. The paralysing spell broken, Elmer Sutton seized his 12-gauge shotgun, quickly loaded it, and let the creature have both barrels. The alien was bowled over like a rabbit by the blast, and collapsed in a heap. Cautiously, the Suttons began to move down the steps of the farmhouse, intent on examining the creature. Suddenly, to their utter amazement,

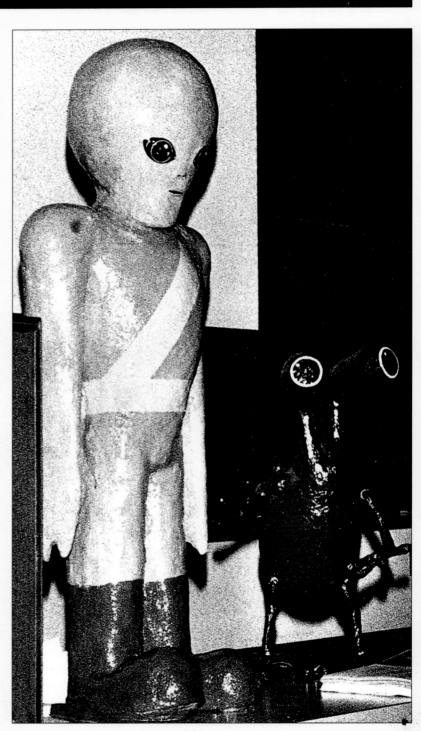

● **BELOW** The Sutton farmhouse was beseiged by aliens four feet (1.22 metres) tall and clad in shiny material – perhaps like this model of an entity named Quazgaa, who featured in an abduction case involving a woman named Betty Andreasson.

ABOVE On 12 September 1952, three boys encountered something strange at Flatwoods, West Virginia, and made independent drawings of the "monster" they had seen.

it bounded to its feet and loped away into the darkness. Shaken, the Suttons ran back into the house and barred the door. The family – eight in all – crowded into the living-room and switched off the lights, waiting in the gloom to see if anything else would happen.

Suddenly, one of the Suttons' daughters gave a piercing scream as she glanced through the open door of the dining-room. Rushing in, the men saw a nightmare creature clinging to the lattice outside the window, peering into the room with luminous slit eyes. Its head was partly covered by some kind of helmet. Elmer Sutton's shotgun exploded with a deafening crash, and his son John snapped off several rounds with his .22 pistol. Glass shattered and the creature vanished abruptly. John ran to the window and looked out, but could see nothing. Once again, the family retreated into the sitting-room and waited. An unearthly silence hung over the farmhouse. Even the dogs were quiet.

But the barking started again, breaking the stillness. Unable to bear the suspense any longer, Elmer and John went outside, gripping their guns tightly. If they had not been so frightened, the sight that met their eyes would have been almost amusing. Among the branches of a tree a few yards away sat one of the strange creatures, and baying around the tree-trunk were Elmer Sutton's dogs.

Before Elmer could do anything, his son gave a shout of alarm. Swinging around, his father saw a second alien crawling along the roof of the house. Taking split-second aim, Elmer loosed off his shotgun. He heard the charge strike the alien with a metallic clang. The thing fell off the roof and hit the ground with a thud, then scrambled up and made a dash for the shadows. As it ran, John hammered away at it with his automatic pistol, hearing the bullets strike home and then whine off into the darkness.

The creature vanished, and the Suttons turned their attention to its companion, still effectively trapped by the snarling dogs. Elmer turned his shotgun on it and blew it off its perch. It fell out of the tree and darted away among the undergrowth. The dogs fled in the opposite direction and cowered under the verandah of the farmhouse.

The next few hours passed uneventfully. It began to look as though the aliens might have had enough

and pulled out of the vicinity. But Elmer decided to take no chances. Loading his family into the station wagon, he drove to the sheriff's office in Hopkinsville, eight miles (13km) away, and reported what had happened. The sheriff listened sceptically to his story, but sent a couple of officers out to the farmhouse to investigate. But the only evidence they found that something out of the ordinary had taken place was one shattered window, a few shot-holes in the wooden walls of the farmhouse, and eight very frightened people.

There was no doubt that the Suttons really were terrified, but just what it was that had frightened them on that August night – aliens bent on kidnapping them for analysis, or something else – remains a mystery. Still, it is tempting to think that on some far planet, there is a race of four-foot (1.2m) humanoids whose emissaries once returned from Earth with the news that the natives were definitely hostile.

● **INSET ABOVE**
Louise Smith made this drawing of an alien she saw during an abduction in Kentucky, USA, 1976. She said that the creature wore a dark hood and a dark suit, and had grey hands.

● **MAIN PICTURE**
Supposed UFO entity photographed by Police Chief Officer Jeff Greenhaw at Falkville, Alabama, on 17 October 1973. Greenhaw had answered a call from a woman who said she had seen a UFO land west of the town. The subsequent publicity cost him both his job and his wife.

● **INSET LEFT** These hieroglyphics were allegedly seen etched on the door of a UFO that abducted Antonio Villas Boas from near his home in Brazil, on 15 October 1975.

# "The end of the world is nigh"

Many stories of alien contact and abduction over the years have had an "end-of-the-world" theme. Adamski, for instance, claimed that his alien friends had given him a special mission: he was to become the new Master whose task was to save the world from self-destruction.

The idea that humanity was about to blow itself to bits was enhanced in the 1950s by the escalating nuclear arms race between East and West, and by the fact that the millenium was only half a century away. People turned up their copies of Nostradamus and other sages and, sure enough, found "proof" that the world would end sometime around 1999. (It was supposed to end in 999, too, but failed to oblige.)

It was rather comforting to think that benevolent beings from outer space were keeping a watch on us, and that they had representatives on Earth who would swing into action to save the world if things showed signs of getting really out of hand. The Earth would then become part of a great Galactic Federation, in which dozens – maybe hundreds – of inhabited planets existed in harmony with one another, and in which Earthlings would become Space Brethren.

First of all, though, we would have to overcome a strong force of evil beings bent on thwarting these happy aspirations – sinister men in black suits who drive around in black limousines threatening, kidnapping and occasionally murdering those people who wanted to save our world.

If all this sounds rather familiar, could it be because it is nothing more than an extension of a theme that formed the plot of many books, films and television series in the 1950s and 1960s, as well as featuring in the press – the long-standing clandestine war between the Central Intelligence Agency, the FBI and Russia's KGB?

RIGHT A UFO beaming down a ray of light into a reservoir in Pennsylvania, 1961. Similar beams of light, or radiation, are often associated with UFO abduction cases.

# UFOs in history

The search for UFO sightings, or evidence that alien space travellers have visited Earth in ancient times, covers a very broad canvas and has given rise to some startling claims. Sodom and Gomorrah were destroyed by alien spacecraft launching nuclear missiles; the walls of Jericho were knocked down by ultrasonic sound waves beamed down from on high; the Great Pyramid was designed with the help of advanced information supplied by extra-terrestrial engineers, and so on.

## The ancient site of Nazca, Peru

One of the favourite hunting-grounds for "evidence" of extra-terrestrial visits is Peru, and in particular the ancient site near Nazca, where patterns of strange lines cover an area of 200 square miles (518km$^2$) between the Pacific Ocean and the Andes Mountains. First discovered by Spanish explorers in the 16th century, the lines spread out in all directions, carved into the rocky surfaces. They depict all manner of geometric shapes, intermingled with huge drawings of animal figures including birds, a spider, a lizard, a snake, a whale, a monkey and a llama. There is also the figure of a man with a halo. Some of the figures are over 900 feet (275m) long, others less than 100 feet (30m).

Serious investigation into the lines began about 50 years ago, when airline pilots started to use them for navigation. Archaeologists travelled to Peru to survey the lines, and to find out more about the long-dead civilization that had carved them into the landscape. The Nazca Indians were a race who inhabited Peru 2,000 years ago, before the Incas – but no one knows for certain whether they carved the lines, or whether they were formed by an even earlier race. The patterns could be as much as 8,000 years old.

According to UFO addicts, the purpose of the curious lines is clear; they formed a kind of navigational beacon that enabled alien spacecraft to home in on Peru when they visited the Nazcas, their occupants imparting much valuable know-

ledge to the natives. The latest theory, advanced by modern science, is much more plausible: the lines were designed as an astronomical calendar, the figures aligned to predict the annual positions of the sun, moon, planets and stars. They were used to predict the correct time of year for planting seeds, harvesting crops and the appearance of water each year in the region's rivers. In this respect, they served the purpose supposed to be the reason for Britain's Stonehenge.

The intriguing aspect, however, is how the intricate patterns were surveyed in the first place, and how the ancient designers were able to retain a fantastic degree of accuracy over great distances. The lines can only be seen in their true perspective from the air, a fact that has long sustained the UFO theory. But lately, scientists have put forward a new notion: the ancient surveyors may have built and flown primitive hot-air balloons. This idea was first projected by an American scientific team, investigating some odd pits that lay close to the end of the lines. The circular pits were blackened by fire, and were just about the right diameter to fit the base of a Montgolfier-type hot-air balloon. Investigating further, the scientists took another look at scraps of linen found in Nazcan tombs, and found that the weave was much tighter than that of the material used to make the envelopes of 18th-century balloons. So the researchers decided to build their own balloon, using the materials the Nazcans might have used, including reeds to build the gondola, to find out if the idea worked.

To their amazement the project was successful. The balloon, designed by American Bill Spohrer, was launched from one of the burn-pits carrying two passengers, Jim Woodman and Julian Knott, both experienced balloonists. Named Condor I, the balloon rose to a height of about 100 feet (30m), but then a sudden downdraught brought it close to the ground again and the two occupants jumped out, thinking it was going to crash. Luckily neither was hurt, and the balloon rose again to a height of over 1,000 feet (300m) and flew for nearly two miles (3km) before coming to earth.

Sadly, no one has been able to prove conclusively that this was the technique originally used to survey the Nazca lines. But the intriguing possibility remains that the ancient Peruvians may have been the first men to learn to fly – with or without extraterrestrial advice.

🔘 **PAGES 59 TO 61**
The so-called "Nazca Lines" in Peru have baffled scientists for many years. First discovered by Spanish explorers in the 16th century, they depict all manner of geometric shapes intermingled with huge drawings of animal figures. The patterns, it is thought, could only have been aligned through aerial observation, and one theory is that the ancient race that carved them used primitive hot-air balloons. According to UFO devotees, the lines formed a kind of navigational beacon that enabled alien spacecraft to home in on Peru in the distant past.

# Out of place artefacts

A continuing underlying theme behind alleged alien contact with Earth in ancient times is the advanced knowledge that some ancient civilizations appear to have possessed. Ever since archaeologists first dug their spades into ancient sites, they have been turning up strange objects that cannot be explained – objects bearing an uncanny resemblance to items that can only be produced by modern technology.

And because they could not be explained rationally such objects have since been tucked away in the dark recesses of museums all over the world, forgotten by everyone except a handful of writers who have tried to prove that they are the remnants of long-lost civilizations. Scientists know them as OOPARTS – Out Of Place Artefacts – and are today attempting to solve their mysteries once and for all.

**BELOW** This object, drawn in 1493 by Hermann Schaden, bears an uncanny resemblance to the black monolith in the film of Arthur C. Clark's science fiction novel, *2001 – A Space Odyssey*, and its sequel, *2010*.

**LEFT** This artefact, discovered in Iraq near Baghdad in 1936, is said to be a 1,800-year-old electric cell. When tested by scientists, it produced a current of up to two volts.

Already, investigators have come up with some astonishing results. In 1936, for example, archaeologists unearthed a strange object from the ruins of a village near Baghdad; it was a clay jar, containing a cylinder of sheet copper with an iron rod suspended in its centre. Since then, similar objects have been found at other sites in Iraq. The original jar and its contents were put on display in the Cairo Museum, Egypt. On several occasions, people who saw it remarked that it looked just like an electric cell. Proof again, said the Ufologists, of technical knowledge passed on by space travellers.

Oddly enough, no one tried to prove that it could be an electric cell until 1976, when a team of German scientists from Hildesheim built an exact replica and, as an acid substitute, filled it with grape juice. There was no longer any doubt that it was an electric battery, for it produced a current of up to two volts in strength. Yet the original battery may be as much as 2,000 years old. So where did the ancient race who lived near what is now Baghdad obtain the knowledge to build it, and for what purpose was it used?

No one, as yet, can answer the first question, but the Germans think they might have an answer to the second. In an experiment, they immersed a small silver statue in a gold cyanide solution and passed an electric current from their model battery through it. In just a couple of hours, the process had given the statue a thin layer of gold. The inference is that ancient goldsmiths used electric current to electroplate their valuables.

Another mysterious object the scientists have worked on is a strange mechanism found in the wreck of a Greek merchant ship that sank in the Aegean sea about 80 BC. Made of bronze and encased in wood, it split into four fragments when it dried out, and the inner surfaces of these fragments were found to contain small, delicate wheels. For a long time, it was thought that the mechanism – discovered in 1900 – was part of an ancient astrolabe, used to calculate the angle of the sun and other celestial bodies. Then, in 1971, scientists investigating the mechanism at America's Yale University took a series of gamma- and X-radiographs of the strange object, and these showed internal details which had not been seen before.

It appeared that the object was not a simple astrolabe, but something far more advanced. It was

LEFT These large black globes were seen over Dasel, Switzerland, on 7 August 1566. The illustration is taken from the Basel Broadsheet of that year, by Samuel Coccius.

a miniature planetarium, using some 30 gears of varying sizes and employing a differential gear system which allowed two shafts to rotate at different speeds. It was to be a thousand years after that Greek ship went down before differential gears were re-invented in the Western world.

In terms of time, that is nothing. Scientists have just discovered that strange markings, carved on bone tools found throughout Europe, represent the phases of the moon – not just as they were when primitive man observed them, but as they would be when the seasons changed. Those bone tools are 30,000 years old, which has led to a drastic revision of scientific thinking about when man first began to observe the heavens, and record what he saw.

There is also the more famous case of the Saqqara Bird. A wooden bird-like object about five and a half inches (14cm) long, it was discovered among the contents of an Egyptian tomb in 1891 and dated to 200 BC. Recently, aero-engineers have carried out a series of tests on it, and they have reached the conclusion that whoever built it, whether as a child's toy or the model for some bigger craft that was never built, must have had a considerable knowledge of aeronautics. The object's wings and fuselage show aerodynamic characteristics and refinements that could not have been stumbled upon accidentally by someone just setting out to carve a toy bird. And it flies, too – perfectly, just like a model glider.

The question is, if the ancient Egyptians had the knowledge to build a model glider such as this, why did they not progress to build a full-size flying-machine? A possible answer is that they might have done, and we don't know about it. Unfortunately, most of the knowledge of the ancient world was stored in the famous library of Alexandria, and

BELOW LEFT A man-built "UFO" in Chinese history: the flying chariot of Ki Kung. This illustration dates from the Sung Dynasty (990-179 AD). The idea is probably based on the man-carrying kites that were used by the Chinese for observation purposes during this period.

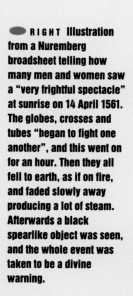

RIGHT Illustration from a Nuremberg broadsheet telling how many men and women saw a "very frightful spectacle" at sunrise on 14 April 1561. The globes, crosses and tubes "began to fight one another", and this went on for an hour. Then they all fell to earth, as if on fire, and faded slowly away producing a lot of steam. Afterwards a black spearlike object was seen, and the whole event was taken to be a divine warning.

lost forever when this was burned down by the Romans in AD 391. Parts of the library had been destroyed before, but on this occasion its greatest treasure – its priceless manuscript collection – was wiped out.

Some scientists believe that the lost knowledge may have held the answer to another big puzzle: how the ancients managed to move huge blocks of stone hundreds of miles to build their great monuments. Recent scientific investigation has shown that the molecular structure of some stones has been altered, leading to the theory that ancient civilizations may have known how to liquify them by chemical means, turning them into a kind of plastic for ease of transportation and then reconstituting them in moulds at the building site. The idea is not entirely fanciful. The Huanca Indians of Bolivia still make stone objects by liqui-fying rock on a small scale with oxalic acid, extracted from rhubarb leaves and other plants. Perhaps the process they use is a dim memory of a much greater one, used on a world-wide scale thousands of years ago.

These are just a few examples of the degree of knowledge that was apparently possessed by the ancient world, and subsequently lost. The question of whether fabled civilizations such as that of Atlantis, armed with vast scientific knolwedge, really existed, is outside the scope of this book. But supposing they did, where did their knowledge come from? The legends of the ancients are filled with tales of flying-machines and other things which equate with our present state of knowledge; it is, perhaps, stretching the imagination a little too far to believe that mankind could have reached such an advanced stage of technical development, unaided, many thousands of years ago.

The main difficulty in analysing this matter, especially in the context of possible extra-terrestrial contact, is to divide tenuous fact – or at least reasonable supposition – from obvious fiction. Many of the "ancient texts", purporting to provide references to such contact, simply never existed; they were the invention of 20th-century writers. Or, if some sort of basic text did exist, it was deliberately doctored to convey the impression that it referred in part to UFO sightings, weapons of mass destruction and so on. It may be that the key to the mystery of whether Earth was visited by extra-terrestrials at the dawn of history lies wait-ing to be discovered. But it will take a mighty scientific wind of discovery to blow away the smokescreen that has been laid over the years by unscrupulous charlatans.

# The search for other worlds

## The case of Epsilon Eridani and Gamma Cephei

Stripping aside the more bizarre stories about "flying saucers", but assuming that UFOs really are alien spacecraft manned by intelligent beings, the leading question then has to be, "Where do they come from?" The search for life beyond the Solar System has been going on for a long time, and Canadian astronomers have come up with the best evidence so far that some of the stars closest to our own Sun may have their own planetary systems. Over a period of six years in the 1980s, the astronomers Bruce Campbell, Gordon Walker and Stephenson Yang made observations of 14 stars from the observatory at Mauna Kea, Hawaii.

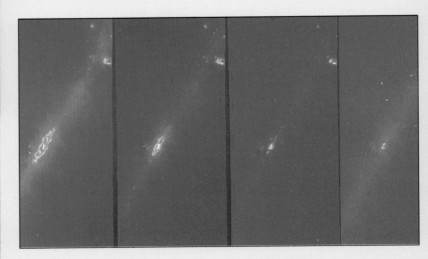

The method they used was to measure the speed of the stars to an accuracy of 25mph (40kmh), and log any regular variations in it. Astronomers already know that fluctuations in a star's speed, or periodic "wiggles" in its path, are a sure indication that it has an unseen companion – either a smaller, invisible star or one or more large planets.

The Canadians believe they have located planets orbiting two nearby sun-type stars, Epsilon Eridani and Gamma Cephei. Epsilon Eridani lies in the long, straggling constellation of Eridanus, which extends from the far south as far as Orion in the

**ABOVE** These four images show the galactic centre of the Milky Way. The plane of the Galaxy appears as the bright diagonal band running from lower left to upper right in each picture. The images were produced from data transmitted by the Infra-red Astronomical Satellite (IRAS).

northern hemisphere. The closest star to us which resembles our own Sun, it is just under 11 light years distant, which means that an object travelling at the speed of light – 186,000 miles (299,274km) per second – would take 11 years to reach it.

The astronomers think that Epsilon Eridani has at least one large planet – bigger even than Jupiter, the largest planet in our own Solar System – and possibly several more smaller ones. The same is apparently true of Gamma Cephei, which is 48 light years away. To find it, locate the Pole Star and look for the brightest star that is closest to it: that is Gamma Cephei. Although similar in mass to our own Sun, it gives out eight times more light, so despite its distance from us it is easier to see than Epsilon Eridani. Of the other stars investigated, the Canadian astronomers say cautiously that five might have planets, although the evidence is not as strong as it is in the case of Epsilon Eridani and Gamma Cephei.

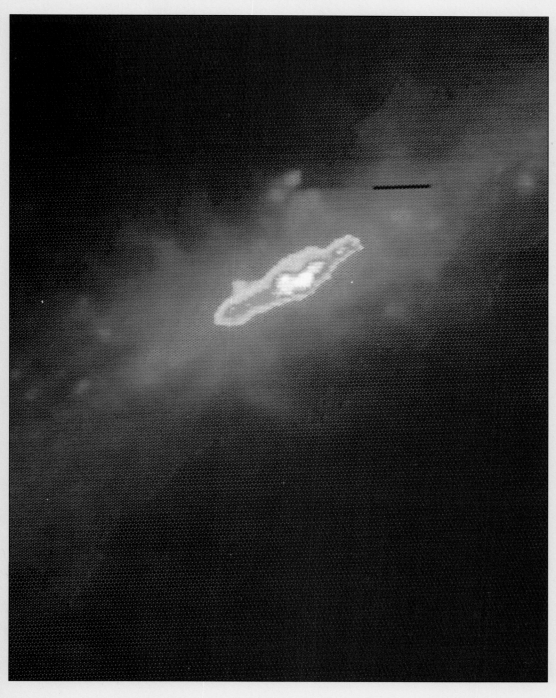

LEFT In this IRAS false-colour image of the Milky Way galactic centre, black represents the dimmest regions of infra-red emission, with blue the next dimmest and red and white the brightest. For the first time, IRAS revealed many details like the streamers of dust around the galactic centre.

# Project Ozma and SETI

The original search for extra-terrestrial life, known as Project Ozma, was pioneered by American astronomer Frank Drake of Cornell University, who began the quest in 1960 with the aid of radio telescopes. Since that time, despite many exciting moments when Drake's team of radio astronomers thought they had tuned in to signals from outer space, only to find that they were false alarms triggered by man-made satellites and radio sources from Earth, there has been no firm evidence to show that mankind has any companions anywhere else in the universe. In the end, Congress decided that the whole project was costing too much money, and closed it down.

Despite the closure of Project Ozma, however, some American astronomers refused to admit defeat. In 1982, 200 US and Soviet scientists met at Tallinn, Estonia, to discuss the chances of continuing the search for life in outer space during the years to come. The renewed quest was known as SETI – Search for Extra-Terrestrial Intelligence – and the initiative for getting it under way came from the Soviet Academy of Sciences.

● **LEFT** Frank Drake, who was in charge of Project Ozma – the search for radio transmissions from alien civilizations. The project, centred on the National Radio Astronomy at Green Bank, West Virginia, was named for the queen of the imaginery land of Oz.

● **BELOW** More than 20 years on, Frank Drake is seen beside pictures of *Voyager*, the spacecraft that gave mankind its first stunning close-up glimpses of the outer planets of the solar system.

# Soviet investigations led by Josef Kardashev

Unlike the Americans, the Russians showed no sign of abandoning the search for intelligent life beyond our planet. In fact, they have striven constantly to improve their techniques in this field of research. At Samarkand, for example, an array of 100 radio telescopes, each with a dish three feet (1m) in diameter, eavesdrops constantly on star systems in selected areas of the northern sky in the hope of detecting artificial signals among the tremendous background clutter of radio noise that fills the universe, while part of the programme of the nearby 230-foot (70m) radio telescope, one of the newest of its kind in the Soviet Union, is devoted exclusively to listening for intelligent signals from the stars.

A firm believer in the possibility that we will one day establish contact with an alien civilization, and one of the leading theorists behind the Soviet programme, is Academician Josef Kardashev, who claims that the level of advancement of such a civilization depends on the amount of energy it uses.

A "Type One" civilization, Kardashev says, is one that makes full use of all the energy that reaches the surface of its planet from whatever sun it orbits. We, on Earth, are on the threshold of attaining this level, with our growing use of solar power and other natural resources.

A "Type Two" civilization has the ability to capture and harness all the energy output of its neighbouring star and control it completely; for example, prevent the star from exploding.

A "Type Three" civilization, according to Kardashev, would be so advanced that it could control the destinies of entire galaxies, destroying stars and building new ones at will. The beings of such a civilization might themselves be composed of pure energy.

Kardashev believes that, instead of looking for mere radio signals, astronomers should concentrate on searching for massive and unexplained releases of energy within the Milky Way Galaxy, which contains our Solar System, and galaxies beyond it. Such bursts of energy could be the "signature" of distant races carrying out undreamed-of feats of space engineering. It may even be, Kardashev says, that supernovas (exploding stars) are the work, at least in some cases, of "Type Three" civlizations.

Already, radio astronomers have investigated well over a thousand stars in their search for intelligent life, and have found nothing. But a thousand stars, as Kardashev points out, is only the tip of the cosmic iceberg: just one-millionth of one

● **BELOW** For many years, the planet Mars was thought to be capable of supporting life – until America's Mariner space probes revealed it to be a barren, crater-strewn wasteland. This photograph, taken by the later *Viking I* orbiter, shows four Martian volcanoes. The topmost, Olympus, towers to a height of 15 miles (24.14km) and is the largest volcano in the solar system.

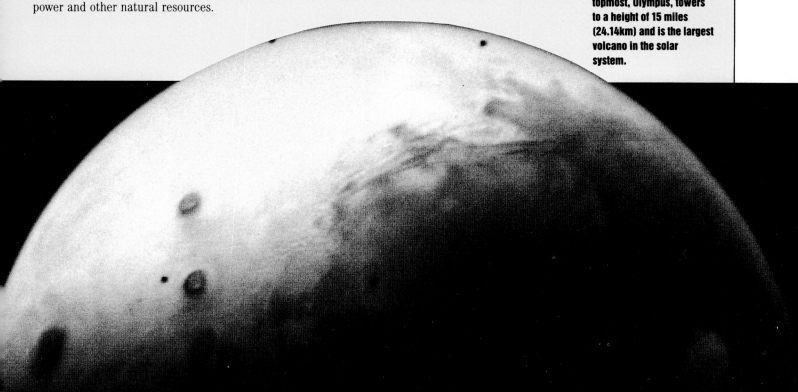

per cent of all the stars in our own Milky Way Galaxy. And beyond that, there are billions more stars in countless other galaxies. Scientists have worked out the odds, and they are formidable. Even if there were a million other civilizations in our galaxy, the odds are that astronomers would have to examine 200,000 star systems before making contact with one of them. The sceptics say that this is a near impossibility. In any case, they state, if there were advanced civilizations in the universe, surely they would have made their presence known already. After all, the Milky Way Galaxy is only 100,000 light years across; an advanced race of space explorers should be able to cross it in about two million years, travelling at one-tenth the speed of light and stopping off to gather information *en route*. Two million years sounds a long time, but the galaxy is 5,000 times older.

● LEFT This artist's impression depicts the first *Viking* mission to Mars. The *Viking* landers took samples of Martian soil and analysed them for traces of life. They found nothing.

# Bob Dixon of the US – a firm believer

One man who does not agree with the sceptics is astronomer Bob Dixon of Ohio State University, who at the 1982 Tallinn conference presented his Soviet counterparts with a specially designed "Flag of Earth". It depicts the Sun, Earth and Moon on a black background. For years, Dixon has continued to carry out a sky search with the help of a team of volunteers in an operation run literally on a shoestring budget. He believes that he has already received an artificial message from the stars.

It happened in August 1977, when his radio telescope was turned towards the constellation Sagittarius. For a few seconds, his instrument received a mysterious radio signal which was recorded on the computer print-out. It was never picked up again, but Dixon remains convinced that it was an intelligent signal originating in deep space.

● LEFT Ever hopeful, a group of UFO enthusiasts set up their "space watch" equipment in a London suburb. Such groups meet frequently in the hope that they will sight UFOs and establish contact with their occupants. One day, maybe they will.

# The birth of radio

While Tesla was blasting the sky with his man-made lightning, another young scientist named Marconi was tapping out the letter "V" in code on his primitive wireless transmitter – and, for the first time, the signal was picked up by Marconi's colleagues 50 miles (80km) away on their receiving apparatus. Two years later, Marconi tapped out the letter "S", and it was picked up on the other side of the Atlantic. The age of the radio was born.

Twenty-two years later, in June 1921, radio stations all over the world reported that they were picking up mysterious signals that appeared to be coming from some point out in space. Strangest of all, the signals were all the same: Marconi's letter "V" in code. In 1924, more strange signals came streaming in – the letter "S" – 22 years since Marconi had flashed his "S" across the Atlantic.

Also in 1924, scientists at a US Navy observatory made a startling disclosure. In August that year the planet Mars approached to within 35 million miles (56 million km) of Earth, and the scientists had been assigned the task of trying to intercept any intelligent signals that might come from the planet. For the job, they used a special camera containing a roll of sensitized paper that passed under a spot of light. The light was in fact a convected radio signal, and the idea was that any message from space would in this way be recorded on the photographic paper.

The scientists operated their "radio camera" for a period of 29 hours, and when the resulting film was developed, they got a surprise. Down one side of the film there was a regular series of dots and dashes. Down the opposite side were what appeared to be several meaningless clusters of dots – until the scientists examined them more closely. Each cluster appeared to represent a crude picture of a human face. For a few weeks, scientific circles talked about practically nothing else. But, unable to resolve it, they filed it away and forgot it.

Two sets of strange messages from space, each one coming just 22 years after Marconi had sent out his first primitive wireless signals. Coincidence perhaps, but there was no escaping the fact that each set of signals had been identical with the code letter tapped out by Marconi nearly a quarter of a century earlier.

The more traditionally minded scientist dismissed the whole business as a hoax, or else ignored it altogether. Others, however, attempted a rational explanation. Suppose that Marconi's early signals, weak though they were, had been amplified by some freak of nature and that they had arrowed out into deep space at the speed of light to be picked up by some super-power receiver? Suppose that whoever picked them up sent out an identical reply almost immediately – a reply that reached Earth 22 years after Marconi's experiments? Half of 22 is 11, so on their outward journey Marconi's signals must have reached a destination that is 11 light-years away in space: the exact distance, from Earth, of the star Epsilon Eridani.

● **BELOW** Marconi seen in 1901 with the transmitting and receiving equipment with which he carried out his early radio experiments. Were his signals picked up by an extra-terrestrial intelligence?

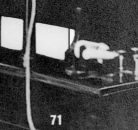

# People like us?

You do not have to be an expert to identify it. It is the third-brightest star in the sky, and on a summer's night it lies directly overhead, shining with a lovely blue colour. Its name is Vega, and it is the chief star of the constellation Lyra. In 14,000 years' time it will be the Pole Star, and by then it may be more important to us than anything else in the heavens. For what is happening around Vega now is a reflection of how our own Sun's family of planets formed billions of years ago.

Until recently, Vega, which is very hot and is 50 times more luminous than the sun, was the last place astronomers thought of looking in their search for life elsewhere in the universe. Vega is 26 light

years away from us, and earlier searches were concentrated on the nearer stars. The first indication that Vega might be the most interesting object in the sky came from IRAS – the Infra-red Astronomy Satellite – whose findings are studied by the scientists of America's Jet Propulsion Laboratory. Because of its brightness, Vega was used to test the sensitivity of IRAS's instruments – and the scientists got more than they had bargained for.

Vega was emitting long-wave radiation, which is associated with relatively cool objects, instead of the short waves the scientists had been expecting. They examined every possible factor that might be causing this puzzling behaviour, and abandoned them all except one. They concluded that Vega must be surrounded by a "shell" of dense material which was blocking out some of its radiation emissions. The scientists estimate the shell of planetary material around Vega to be about twice the diameter of our own Solar System. What they do not yet know is how far the process of planetary evolution out there may have advanced. It may only just be starting, or planets, some the size of Jupiter, may already have formed and be capable of sustaining life.

**ABOVE AND BELOW** This UFO was photographed by schoolboy Dima Girenko on 4 February 1990 near the settlement at Solnechnoye in the Ukraine. According to analysts at the Moscow Aviation Institute, the photos are not faked. One photograph shows the UFO apparently with landing gear extended.

**OPPOSITE** Definitely *not* like us, this creature allegedly came from a UFO that crashed near Mexico City in the 1950s. It was sent to Germany for examination and, predictably, turned out to be a hoax.

# Our own Solar System and Earth

Our own Sun was once surrounded by such a shell of cosmic matter. As billions of years went by, it cooled down and coalesced into the planets we know so well, including our own Earth. This occurred some 4,500 million years ago. The planets nearest the Sun – Mercury, Venus, Earth and Mars – were subjected to the greatest heat and lost most of their lighter, gaseous elements to become solid, rocky spheres with thin atmospheric layers (a very tenuous one in Mercury's case). Further out, where things were cooler, lightweight elements could condense out in gaseous compounds capable of being held together by gravity. The result was the four "gas giant" planets – Jupiter, Saturn, Uranus and Neptune. The Solar System's ninth planet, Pluto, is almost certainly an escaped moon that did not originate as a planet.

Of all these worlds, Earth is the only one with water and an oxygen-rich atmosphere, ideal conditions for the breeding and sustaining of life. Orbiting in the narrow zone between fire and ice, its atmospheric shield is just right to keep the surface of the planet hotter than the freezing-point of water and cooler than its boiling-point. The result is a wet planet, where water continuously evaporates from the oceans and is recycled as rain. So how did these perfect conditions arise, and could they conceivably be repeated elsewhere?

When the Sun settled down into the steady state of activity that has lasted for the past 4.6 billion years, gases seeped out from the interiors of the inner planets to form their present atmospheres.

This so-called "outgassing" came from cooling rocks, from volcanic activity and from vaporization that occurred when large meteorites hit the surface at high velocity. Ultraviolet radiation from the Sun interacted with gases such as methane, ammonia, molecular hydrogen and water vapour to produce atmospheric molecules that are now widely accepted as the precursors of life.

Initially, the surface temperature on Earth before this "outgassing" process began would have been low, about ($-45°C$), but it later became warmer – hot enough for liquid water to flow but not so high that large quantities of water vapour got into the atmosphere to produce a runaway "greenhouse" effect. This was checked by carbon dioxide, dissolved out of the atmosphere by the warming waters. The temperature rose somewhat, but eventually settled down to an average of around $59°F$ ($15°C$).

Conditions were not yet quite right for the beginning of life on the Earth's surface; lethal quantities of ultraviolet radiation still blasted out of the Sun. In the oceans, however, these harmful rays were filtered out, providing a safe haven for life to develop. Life emerged, and soon began to play its part in shaping Earth's environment.

The first life-forms found oxygen poisonous, a dangerous waste product of their life processes, but after around two billion years of evolution oxygen produced by these creatures was beginning to build up in the atmosphere, where chemical reactions stimulated by the Sun's radiation led to the production of ozone high in the atmosphere.

This formed a layer, effectively filtering out much of the harmful ultraviolet, and under its protection life slowly began to emerge from the sea – life that thrived on oxygen as an energy source.

There are billions of Sun-type planets in our galaxy, all of them bound to have a "life zone" – an area around them, millions of miles in extent, in which an Earth-type planet could generate conditions favourable not only for producing life, but life as we know it. If the experiment of Earth's evolutionary process could be repeated, the same lifeforms would almost certainly evolve, perhaps with minor variations.

# Intelligent life elsewhere and black holes

**RIGHT This UFO appeared in a photograph of a giraffe taken at Plymouth Zoo, Devon, England, by Wilfred Power, in 1972. The photographer observed nothing out of the ordinary at the time.**

The process of evolution in our galaxy leads to a comforting supposition. It is that wherever stars like our Sun exist, there ought to be planets like the Earth in orbit around them, with the basic ingredient of life – water – flowing freely on their surfaces. In which case, there will be oxygen, blue skies, plants and animals. If there is intelligent life on such worlds, it will not be in the form of bug-eyed, reptilian monsters beloved of science-fiction writers; the "aliens", in all probability, will be people very much like ourselves.

But supposing such races, more advanced than our own, are capable of interstellar travel, how do they achieve it? Even a spacecraft capable of attaining velocities approaching the speed of light would take years to bridge the gulf between neighbouring stars. There must be another, less obvious way.

Amos Ori, of the California Institute of Technology, says that black holes might provide a gateway to other universes through tunnels in space-time. His theory is that quantum effects may make it possible to "tunnel" through the surface surrounding a black hole and emerge into another region of space and time. Physicists have known for more than half a century that the mathematical description of a black hole in ordinary space portrays the hole as a kind of tunnel, or bridge, connecting two separate regions of flat space. Albert Einstein carried out some of the pioneering calculations along these lines.

For many years, theorists regarded these space-time tunnels as simply a quirk of mathematics, with no physical significance. Recently, however, several theorists have become intrigued by the possibility that such tunnels through the fabric of space-time might exist. The snag with this theory is the so-called blue sheet problem. The boundary, or horizon, of a black hole is a surface where the pull of gravity is so strong that nothing, not even light, can escape. One way of interpreting this is to say that light leaving the horizon is infinitely "red shifted" to zero energy; this means that light falling on to the horizon from outside must be infinitely "blue shifted", piling up to form an energetic "blue sheet" around the hole.

Theorists used to think that this blue sheet would form an impenetrable barrier, but Ori has shown that objects approaching it may not necessarily be destroyed. The key question is whether tidal forces are strong enough to tear an object apart near the critical horizon. According to Ori's calculations, they are not. The barrier exists, but it simply cannot be crossed.

**LEFT The strange phenomena of space have often been confused with UFOs.**

# The unexplored mysteries of space

Terrestrial science is just beginning to come to grips with the mysteries of space and time. The achievements of space scientists in the past half-century have been impressive enough; they have put men on the Moon, placed robot landers on Mars and Venus, photographed the outer planets from close range – all with the raw power of liquid-fuelled rockets.

Starship designs are already on the drawing-board, but they all rely on existing power technology. The British Interplanetary Society, for example, has already proposed a spacecraft design for an unmanned mission to Barnard's Star, which is 5.8 light years away and which may have a planetary system. Known as Project Daedalus, the spacecraft would be powered by the fusion of deuterium pellets ignited by a laser 250 times a second. The result would be a series of pulsed micro-explosions in a magnetically insulated thrust chamber.

The 620-foot-long (189m) Daedalus would have to be assembled in Earth orbit. Its fusion engine would boost it to a speed of 10 and 20 per cent of the speed of light over a period of several years, during which it would use up all its main engine fuel. The spent fuel tanks would be jettisoned and Daedulus would then coast through interstellar space for the rest of its one-way trip to Barnard's Star, which would last up to 50 years. To protect it against high-speed impacts with particles during its journey, Daedalus would be fitted with a large, flat shield at its bow. However, the craft would be travelling so fast that a collision with an object with a mass of only one gramme would be enough to destroy it. So its designers have come up with a "Dust Bag", a robot that precedes the main craft at a distance of 120 miles (190km) and emits a cloud of dust particles that would vaporize bodies weighing up to half a ton (508kg).

As it approaches the Barnard's Star system, Daedalus would launch up to 20 probes to fly by any nearby planets, gathering information. The whole operation would be controlled by the spacecraft's computers, because signals from Earth would take years to reach it. That is the biggest snag to the whole project. By the time Daedalus had gathered its information and transmitted it back to Earth, a young scientist involved in the launching would probably be a great-grandfather.

Crude though they are, craft such as Daedalus represent a step along the road to the stars, a form of intermediate progress until other, more exotic propulsion systems are devised, as they surely will be. It may be, as UFO adherents would like to believe, that the stars will come to us in the meantime. If they do not, then one day the human race, embarking on its greatest adventure, will go to them. And then we shall know at last whether we are alone, an accident of fate in the vastness of the Universe – or whether the intolerable burden of loneliness will be forever lifted from the shoulders of mankind.

● ABOVE This site at Cradle Hill, Warminster, Wiltshire, has been the scene of many alleged UFO sightings. This corner of England has long been famous for strange happenings.

● RIGHT The second stage of the starship Daedalus is photographed here during the lengthy testing operations in a manoeuvre in Uranus space.

# Index

(References to illustrations are in *italics*)

## A

Adamski, George 50–2, *50, 51,* 57
Aegean Sea 64
Aerial Phenomena Research
    Organization 15
aircraft shadowed by UFOs 11, 15, 19, *19,*
    45–6, *47,* 49
Alexandria, library of 64–5
aliens 9, 10, 24, 31–3, 43, 50–1, 52, 53,
        54–6, *54, 55, 56,* 66, *73,* 75
    contact with 13, 15, 31–3, 50–6, 57,
        58–60, 62–5
    descriptions of 31, 53, 54–5
Alves, Raul 39
Arctic Circle 38
Arnold, Kenneth 6, *6, 8,* 16, 42, 50, 51
astronomical calendar 60
Atlantis 65
atmospheric conditions 9, 18, 45, 74–5
attack by UFOs 15, 31–3, 53, 54–6
attempts to explain UFOs 9, 13, 15, 18,
    22–3, 30, 38, 54
attempts to intercept UFOs 16, 46, 48–9
Australia 19, 22

## B

B-29 bomber 11, *11,* 12, 42, 43
Baghdad 63, 64
Bailey, Master Sgt. 11
ball lightning 35, *35*
Barnard's Star 76
Bass Strait 19
battery, 1,800-year-old 63–4, *63*
Bentwaters, Suffolk (USAF base) 48, 49
Bible, the 13
black holes 75
blue sheet 75
Borman, Frank 22–3
Brazel, William 42
Brazil 39–41
Brezhnev, Leonid 27
British Government 38
British Interplanetary Society 76

## C

C-118 aircraft 14–15, *14,* 16
California Institute of Technology 75
Campbell, Bruce 66
Cape Canaveral (Kennedy) 22
Carswell (USAF base) 42
Catalina flying boat 36–7
Cessna 182 aircraft 19
Chance Vought XF5U-1 aircraft, 9, *9*
CIA 57
Cisco, Joe & Dave 29
Clements, Lt. A.W. 17
Cocklin, Howard 12
Coleman, Lt. Sid 11
conditions for life on Earth 74–5
Condor I 60
contact with aliens 13, 50–6, 57, 58–60,
    62–5
Cooper, Maj. Gordon 22
Cornell University 68
Cosmos satellite 24, 25
Covas, Sgt. Alberto 45
cover-ups 15, 18, 22, 30, 38, 42

## D

Daedalus starship 76, *76*
Darnbyl, Col. Gernod 38
DC-4 airliner 12, *12*
de Havilland Venom NF.2 fighter *48,* 49
de Souza, Ruth & Elidia 39
descriptions of UFOs 7, 12, 16, 19, 22, 29,
    30, 37–8, 39–40, 47, 49, 53
differential gears 64
Dixon, Bob 70
Drake, Frank 68, *68*
Dykman, George 28–9

## E

Earth *20,* 70, 71, 74–5, 76
Egyptians, ancient 64
Einstein, Albert 75
"end of the world" 57
Epsilon Eridani 66–7, 71
Eridanus 66
evolution 74–5

## F

F-84 Thunderjet 44–6, *45*
FBI 7
Federal Aviation Administration 49
Ferreira, Capt. Jose 44–6
Ferris, Staff Sgt. 11
"flying saucers" 8, *9,* 10, 13, 25, 26, 30, 37,
    38, 50, 51, *51,* 66
"Foo Fighters" 35, *35*
Fortenberry, W.H., 2nd Off. 12
Fuller, John G., *The Interrupted Journey*
    53

## G

Galactic Federation 57
Gamma Cephei 66–7
Gemini spacecraft 22
Gloster Meteor jet fighter 47
Godman (USAF base) 16
Granada, Spain 45
Great Pyramid 58
Gulf of Mexico 11
Gustafsson, Hans 31–3, 35

## H

Hale Observatory, USA 50
Hammond, Lt. B.A. 17
Harter, Capt. John 11
Hawaii, 22, 66
Hawker Hunter jet fighter 47, *47*
Helsingborg, Sweden 31
Hill, Barney & Betty, 53, *53*
Hoganas, Sweden 81
hot-air balloon 60
Huanca Indians 85
hysteria over UFOs 6, 8, 9, 10, 13, 24, 30,
    43, 50 53

## I

Iguape, Brazil 39
Iovanne, Caetano 41
investigations into UFOs 8, 9, 15, 21, 33,
    38, 41, 48, 49
Iraq 63
IRAS (Infra-red Astronomy Satellite) 73